ALL YOU NEED IS LOVE

...AND 99 OTHER LIFE LESSONS FROM CLASSIC ROCK SONGS

PETE FORNATALE

AND

BILL AYRES

A FIRESIDE BOOK

Published by Simon & Schuster

FIRESIDE
Rockefeller Center
1230 Avenue of the Americas
New York, NY 10020

FIRESIDE and colophon are registered
trademarks of Simon & Schuster Inc.

Designed by MM Design 2000

Manufactured in the United States of America

10 9 8 7 6 5 4 3 2 1

Library of Congress Cataloging-in-Publication Data
Fornatale, Peter.
All you need is love : —and 99 other life lessons from classic rock songs / Pete
Fornatale and Bill Ayres.
p.   cm.
(alk. paper)
1. Conduct of life. 2. Rock music—History and criticism. I. Ayres, Bill. II. Title.
BJ1595.F64 1998
158.1'28—dc 21   98-26296
                                             CIP

ISBN 0-684-84529-6

Cover photograph by Bruce Osborn/Photonica

To our partner

Harry Chapin

who spent the last ten years of his life
taking millions of fans to "a better place to be"
with his touching, wonder-filled story-songs,
and helping millions more to have food in their stomachs,
dignity in their lives, and hope in their spirits.

ACKNOWLEDGMENTS

Bill:

I grew up singing Gregorian Chant, Bach Chorales, Broadway show tunes, and pop standards. Meanwhile, I was voraciously listening to and intoxicated by jazz and the blues. Hearing this new music, rock 'n' roll, it seemed to me to be mostly white people ripping off black music. I did not get it. I loved Chuck Berry and Fats Domino, but it wasn't until I learned to dance as a teenager that I began to *feel* rock 'n' roll. The man who really helped me to get it, however, was my partner Pete Fornatale. I heard this young, just-out-of-college teacher talking about the values of rock music for education back in 1967, at a summer course offered by Fordham on media for teachers. Pete was the opening act, so to speak, for the likes of Sidney Poitier and Marshall McLuhan, but he was the person that really reached me. For the first time, I began to seek out the best in rock and use it in my classes. I also asked Pete to be the cohost for an adventurous radio show I was starting on WGSM in Huntington, Long Island, called *Religion Revisited* that combined rock 'n' roll with religion and spirituality. In 1973 I began a new show called *On This Rock* on the ABC Radio Network and WPLJ-FM in New York where I still host a weekly call-in show. So, my first acknowledgement is to my partner Pete Fornatale, without whom I might still be singing boring pop songs and teaching boring, musicless classes.

I would also like to thank Harry Chapin and Bruce Springsteen, who have shown the world that rock 'n' roll is so much more than self-indulgent, self-important, and self-destructive behavior. Their music and their generosity have been lifegiving to me and to generations of ardent music fans and social activists.

Thanks to Jessica Keith, who accomplished what we two techno-peasants could not, actually putting the text into the computer with loving care. Thanks also to our excellent editor, Becky Cabaza, who gave us great suggestions all along, including her first one, which prevented us from trying an impossible manuscript that would have undoubtedly discouraged us and wound up as "rock folly" instead of "rock wisdom."

Strange as it may seem, I wrote more than 80 percent of my part of *All You Need Is Love* riding to and from work on the Long Island Railroad, that much-maligned but truly wonderful mode of commuter transportation. Think about it—no one to bother you, no interruptions from phone calls, and the wheels of the train that create a gentle motion conducive to creativity.

Finally, I would like to thank my wife Jeannine, who has always encouraged and supported our work and my two other lovely ladies, my daughters Michelle and Suzanne, who are growing up loving the music.

Pete:

My thanks begin with Mark Gompertz for saying yes again, and, to Becky Cabaza for guiding this project every step of the way from conception to bookshelf.

I am indebted to the following people for sharing their journeys of faith with me when I needed them most: Jeannine Ayres, Rose and Curt Boddie, Pat and Jim Brennan, Ann and Jim Coady, Dion DiMucci, Dr. Steven Greenberg, Ruth and Einar Haukeland, Diana and Don Holden, Priscilla and Tom Malone, Camilla and Roger McGuinn, Noel Stookey, Jerry Trombella, and George Vecsey.

Deepest gratitude to my personal and professional brain trust: John Abbracciamento, Irving Block, Mark Chernoff, Dennis Elsas, Dick Hessler, Wayne Kabak, Alan Katz, Paul Kurland, Don McGee, Allan Pepper, John Platt, and Dr. Richard Rabkin.

As always, here's to the home team: my wife Susan and our sons Peter, Mark, and Steven.

Finally, I cannot even imagine having done this book without Bill Ayres. He has been my friend, confidant, spiritual advisor, and partner since 1968. I consider it a gift to be able to celebrate our thirty years of friendship with the publication of *All You Need Is Love*.

CONTENTS

FOREWORD

Only the Lonely

Roy Orbison was more than just a great singer. He sang songs of overwhelming psychological impact, songs that spoke to the heart of the things that draw people to art and music in the first place: the delicious fears expressed in "Running Scared" and "In Dreams," the enchantments of "Leah" and "Blue Bayou," the lusts of "Oh, Pretty Woman" and "Uptown." His are songs of visions and dreams—some fearful, some hopeful, some joyous, some somber. Each of these songs, and above all, his greatest, "Only the Lonely," is anxious and obsessed. Whether the source of these nervous preoccupations is thwarted love in the real world or the shadows in our own heads, or the inability to distinguish one from the other, Orbison's records produce an added force from the delicate power and intricately shaded feelings his voice conveys. Taken together, singer and song achieve a startling universality. You can call it whatever you like, but to me, when Roy Orbison sings, ever so sadly and ever so gently, "Only the lonely know the way I feel tonight," there's an artist at work. And as with all art, if you understand it, the main thing you have to feel is a sense of connection. Who hasn't felt those improbable feelings? Who hasn't been so worried, so depressed? In all that loneliness, isn't it the point that each lonely person feels what all the other lonely people feel? There is a name for this idea in American art—it is called "the blues"—but the particular mode in which Roy Orbison expressed it will be familiar to millions of people who know and care nothing about the blues as a form. It doesn't make any difference—that great connection among all the questing hearts remains.

There are literally hundreds of examples of this kind of connection in rock and pop and soul music—the kinds of music discussed in this book. The fact that these connections exist, and that they are the source of the music's appeal, is the true subject matter of *All You Need Is Love*—and the emphasis here is on "need" as much as on "love." Some parts of it are more about one than the other, of course, and the kinds of love are pretty much as diverse as the varieties of needs these great songs address. But the point is that all such grand and common subjects truly *are* addressed in rock 'n' roll songs. Indeed, it's plain to see that over the past half-century, it has been the songs of our popular music—the rock songs, the R&B and soul songs, the ones that came out of folk and funk—that have been, above any other art, spiritual movement or therapy, the readiest access point to open and honest discussion of such topics in our society. What this book does is amplify what we already know or, at least, what we already suspect; it pulls out of some of the most important songs their most helpful and frightful implications. It is in the tradition of books of "affirmations," and the first thing that it affirms is that such deep content exists. Since the attacks on our popular music as shallow and meaningless, harmful rather than healing, have been unrelenting since its inception in the 1950s, this is a singularly important achievement. It's hard for me to imagine any lover of that music, or any of its offshoots, who doesn't know that this material is embedded in the music. Whether your heart belongs to Prince, the Pretenders, John Prine or Primus, George Clinton or George Harrison, what drew you to the music in the first place was not only a certain face and a certain voice, a specific beat or melody or guitar lick, nor even the approval of your peers or the need to explore something so unfashionable it felt forbidden, it was also the way in which those records filled the needs of your heart and emotions, addressing passions and perils you didn't know had anything to do with you.

Certainly, for everyone to whom rock and soul and funk and folk and rap and punk and all the other offshoots of the original whole and holy amalgam of blues, country, and gospel has had continuing appeal, it is this ability to touch what most needs touching that keeps us coming back.

The information in *All You Need Is Love* gains its importance because it's useful; it's a way of knowing more about the song, and more about its inner spirit. Additionally, the text provides a way of doing something about the needs the songs address. This book proceeds out of a true understanding of rock and related musics, an understanding that could have been conveyed only by people who love them. What Fornatale and Ayres know, it seems to me, is that people already use such songs to sustain and guide them through life. The book exists to help us do it better. In this respect, it is an act of love. The songs you cherish most may or may not be here; I don't think anyone but Pete and Bill will love all of them, but neither will most rock fans feel like they've been altogether shut out. In any event, one of the most important things that *All You Need Is Love* does is provide a true tutorial. When you are done combing its pages, you will be able to apply its methods to whatever song you cherish, and find a new, more complete understanding of it.

I know this for certain because when I got the book, my first impulse was to look for Roy Orbison songs. Some were there, but for me, The One was not: "Only the Lonely" is missing. But after reading the book, I soon realized that it had given me the tools to make more of my passion for the song, what it has to say and the way in which it's said. In this way, Pete Fornatale and Bill Ayres have created a tool that every listener can use, and that is a rare and special thing. I thank them for it.

—Dave Marsh
6/23/98

INTRODUCTION

We began interviewing rock stars on the radio in the late sixties (Pete on WNEW-FM in New York City) and early seventies (Bill on WPLJ-FM in New York City). At the time, most rock interviews consisted of a series of perfunctory questions about the artist's latest tour and album, often just a step above the "what's your favorite color?" genre of inquiry. The interviewing level fell right in with and reinforced the public's perception of the mental and moral acuity of the performers as blithering drug-crazed dummies. Along the way, we may have met our share of folks in the business who fit that description, but most were not artists. Perhaps it is because we have always approached them with a combination of respect and delight but, invariably, the hundreds of interviews we have both done have been intelligent, often revealing, and sometimes quite moving.

There is a kind of integrity in the vast majority of the men and women we have interviewed and, on occasion, true wisdom. Of course, the wisdom is also reflected in their music and we have been touched by it over the past thirty years, again and again. We suspect you have as well, and that from time to time you might have learned a great truth from listening to a favorite song. We are quite aware that's not the primary reason that any of us listen to rock 'n' roll. It's good-time music. It has been our companion in our cars, at parties and dances, and in our otherwise lonely rooms as we grew up. It has helped us to survive adolescence and many of the traumas and tragedies of life. We both celebrate and mourn with it and, sometimes, when we least expect it, a line or a whole song hits us in a way that we remember forever.

All You Need Is Love is both a visit to our past and a companion for our present and future. But, first, a few ground rules. If you are looking for line-by-line explanations or interpretations of the songs listed here, you will have to look elsewhere for that. Our main purpose was to dispel the stereotypical assumption that rock 'n' roll songs were only about sex, drugs, and boogeying all night long. We insist on every page of this book that there is a whole other dimension to this cultural phenomenon that has been a universal touchstone and common language for multiple generations the world over. In some cases, it's the entire song, in other cases it's a line or more of the lyrics and, in still others, it's just the song title that sparks a creative rumination about the human condition which touches the heart, satisfies the thirst and yearning inside each of us, and illustrates the interconnectedness between us all.

We also want to stress that these one-hundred titles are not necessarily our hundred favorites, or the best or most popular songs of all time. We chose them primarily because they all contain opportunities for wisdom, were at one time popular, and are still available on CD. We hope that you will send us your suggestions and choices for rock wisdom that we may have missed this time around.

We have written reflections on the titles, and some suggestions for incorporating the lessons into your life. The insights are the kind that Bill has been sharing with his late night call-in audience on WPLJ-FM for twenty-three years. The introductory comments on the music have been Pete's trademark for more than thirty years on the radio and give information to enhance the listener's enjoyment. And that, dear friends, is what we hope you have with this book, the enjoyment of listening to the songs again, this time with the "third ear" so that the music may touch you anew, and give you the unexpected gift of what we call *Rock Wisdom.*

ALL YOU NEED IS LOVE

...AND 99 OTHER LIFE LESSONS FROM CLASSIC ROCK SONGS

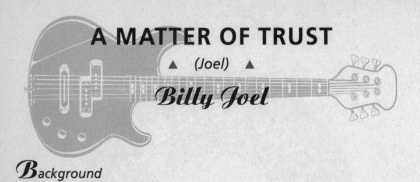

A MATTER OF TRUST
▲ *(Joel)* ▲

Billy Joel

*B*ackground

From the very beginning of his career, Billy Joel was known as the piano man. It wasn't only the title of his breakthrough album and a big hit single, it was also the perfect image for a man who had worked out some of his greatest music at the keyboards, and who never failed to display his dazzling mastery of the instrument in concert. So, in 1986, when Billy strapped on a Stratocaster for his new song "A Matter of Trust," fans sat up and took notice. Was the piano man abandoning his keyboard for the more traditional pose of the guitar hero? Not really. Playing guitar in the video and in concert gave Billy the opportunity to roam the stage more freely, but the actual guitar playing on the track was done by David Brown and Russell Javors. "A Matter of Trust" was released as a single from *The Bridge* album and rose to number ten on the charts.

*R*eflection

Many years ago, a college friend called two nights before his marriage to his high-school sweetheart. They had just had a terrible fight that started with some wedding preparation minutiae, and then went ominously deeper into the darkest corners of their personalities. He said "I thought I knew everything about her after all these years, but I learned things tonight I did not think could possibly be true."

Love is, as Billy Joel says, a matter of trust, and trust does depend on knowing the other deeply. That does not mean having controlling knowledge that can anticipate every thought, every move. Trust is based on touching the mystery in your beloved and being touched in return, which calls for vulnerability in both of you. If you or your partner never reveal yourselves to each other at an intimate level there will be no basis of trust. As you do open yourselves, trust will grow.

It would be wonderful if trust was only that easy. You both keep revealing yourselves, respecting each other for whom you are, and building trust upon trust. In reality, trust is also built on shared pain, disappointments, a series of minor betrayals, and often major betrayals that rock the very foundation of your relationship. All that you have carefully built seems to disappear before your eyes, as in the story of my friend just before his wedding. Then, after the waves of suffering and anxiety pass, you look again with the eyes of love and you can still see love coming back your way. Trust is slowly restored although shadows remain. By the way, our friend did go through with the wedding and, yes, they are still married.

Actions

▲ Trust is essential in all relationships, but especially in that most important of all, the one with your significant other. How would you describe your trust in this relationship: total to near total, strong in some areas but weak in others, or diminishing to minimal?

▲ Trust is not static, it either grows or decreases. What is the state of trust with your partner now? Is it better or worse then this time last year?

▲ Have you already successfully built trust in your relationship? How can you apply some of those well-learned lessons to a problem of trust now?

Album

The Bridge; Billy Joel; Columbia CK 40402.

ABRAHAM, MARTIN AND JOHN
▲ (Holler) ▲
Dion

Background

Dion DiMucci was almost a victim of the British invasion. After years of success and hit records with and without his Bronx-based group, The Belmonts, Dion virtually disappeared from the pop spotlight in the wake of Beatlemania. But, then, in 1968, he reinvented himself as an urban blues/folksinger, and touched a national nerve with Dick Holler's song about assassination called "Abraham, Martin and John". Dion was back on the charts with a hit that climbed to number four in November of 1968. (In a delicious bit of irony, The Beatles paid homage to Dion by including him in the montage of their heroes on the cover of *Sgt. Pepper's Lonely Hearts Club Band*.)

Reflection

I was at a book sale at school, when I heard on the radio that President Kennedy had been shot and was dying. I also remember when I first heard the news of Martin Luther King, Jr. and Bobby Kennedy's deaths. They were not only my heroes but the heroes of my generation, of our whole country. It often seems that courage is rewarded with death, but then, the memory of heroes, the power and goodness of the heroes lives on even after we learn of their tragic flaws.

We grow up believing that our heroes can do no wrong, that there are people, sometimes beginning with our parents, who are nearly perfect. Suddenly or gradually, the bubble bursts and we can become terribly disillusioned, even as adults. Yet the deeds of our heroes remain, their courage remains, and the help that they provided changed the lives of millions for the better.

Heroes are not saints, and even saints are far from perfect. Heroes usually do not set out to be heroes. They do not train for the role. They are there at the right time, and respond to a crisis. They choose, often at great sacrifice and with reluctance, to take a leadership role, and the power of their personalities and actions attracts followers and makes a difference.

Actions

▲ Are there any national or international figures today that you would consider heroes? Who? Why do you believe that they are heroes?

▲ Are there any other national or international figures that you once considered heroes but do not now? Why did you change your mind?

▲ Are there personal heroes from your past or present, people who were role models for you from your family, friends, school, job or some other personal contact? What made them heroes? How have they made a difference in your life?

▲ Do you think you might be a hero or role model for others? What qualities, heroic acts, or long-term dedication might they admire in you?

Album

Dion; Dion; The Right Stuff T2-29667.

ALL THINGS MUST PASS

▲ (Harrison) ▲

George Harrison

Background

Try to imagine being caught in the creative crossfire of John Lennon and Paul McCartney. That was the position that George Harrison found himself in throughout the glory years of the Beatles. In the face of their prolific song-writing, George was lucky to squeeze one, sometimes two, of his own compositions on each new Beatles album. So it should have come as no surprise that when the group disbanded it was George Harrison who exploded into a songwriting frenzy. His first post-Beatles solo effort was the brilliant three-record set *All Things Must Pass,* brimming with hit singles, enduring album tracks, and compassionate ruminations about the human condition, such as "Isn't It A Pity," "The Art of Dying," and the great title song.

Reflection

There is good news and bad news here, as well as news that actually contradicts the title. The good news can be summarized in the parallel phrase "this too shall pass." It is a very comforting and accurate truth that can help you deal with short-term, intense pain and long-term, persistent pain. Remember the feeling of a past suffering, whether physical or emotional, and how it felt as though it would go on forever? Then realize that it is no more. You made it through and you can do it again. There is a way.

The bad news is that the best moments of your life are just that, moments, your greatest successes may pass, and be the seed of failure. The big day, the event you worked so hard for, planned so long for, is here and quickly gone, and now you feel empty rather than fulfilled. Time seems to go by ever more quickly when you hit middle age, and it can suddenly appear that your best years are over.

The seemingly contradictory news is that although on one level all things must pass, on another, still deeper level we do not live only from minute to minute. The past does endure, not just as a distant memory but as a powerful presence in our lives now. A series of career successes, for example, are not simply a haphazard collection of isolated incidents. They are the building blocks of a legitimate sense of pride and accomplishment. Good deeds of justice, charity, and loyalty remain as part of the fabric of our being and help make us who we are. They also form our reputations in the community and inform our relationships with our family, friends, and acquaintances. They are a vital part of the social capital upon which we base our lives. Also, our experiences of celebration, hospitality, prayer, learning, relaxation, exercise, and culture do not disappear from our beings immediately after completion. They, too, are the foundation of our personality.

*A*ctions

▲ If you are in a great deal of pain right now, for any reason, and it has been with you for quite a while, try to remember a past suffering that is gone. How did you handle that one? What helped? Who helped? Is there anything you can do either to get yourself out of the painful situation or learn how to deal with it better?

▲ How can you remember a wonder-filled past experience? Try visualization. Allow yourself to relive your date with that extraordinary person; a great business, cultural, or athletic accomplishment; the presence of a departed loved one; or an intense spiritual experience. Be quiet and allow yourself to experience the joy once more. Often, the original experience was so intense and all-consuming that it is not possible to take it all in on the first try. Visualization can help you to retrieve what may have been lost. One warning: Remember that you cannot live in the past—use this not as a crutch but as a tool to move your life forward.

*A*lbum

All Things Must Pass; George Harrison; Capitol CDP 7 46688 2.

ALL YOU NEED IS LOVE

▲ *(Lennon/McCartney)* ▲

The Beatles

*B*ackground

On June 1, 1967, The Beatles released *Sgt. Pepper's Lonely Hearts Club Band*. Since they wanted the entire album to be treated as a whole, the decision was made not to release any of the individual tracks as singles. Instead, the group participated in a worldwide, satellite-television broadcast on June 25, 1967, called *Our World*. The Beatles were shown recording a song written especially for the event, entitled "All You Need Is Love." The result was released as a single a week later and immediately shot to the top of the charts all over the world. It also instantly became the anthem for the so-called Summer of Love.

*R*eflection

In a recent interview for *The Beatles Anthology*, Paul McCartney recalled how much of the group's music revolved around the subject of love. He concluded by commenting specifically about "All You Need Is Love," "I'm very proud to be in the band that did that song and thought those thoughts and that encouraged many people to think them. . . . we done good!" We certainly agree. "All You Need Is Love" very neatly and succinctly sums up the message of the Beatles, and it also very neatly and succinctly sums up the message of rock wisdom. Love *is* all you need to navigate through this obstacle course that is life on earth.

Each day of our lives, almost each moment of our existence, we have to make a choice between acting from some part of us deep inside that is loving, compassionate, caring, and considerate, or from some part of us deep inside that is fearful, angry, distrustful, and selfish. Often, our defense mechanisms are so rigidly in place that we automatically opt for the latter responses. Some people have the rare gift of constantly being able to put love in the front of their consciousness in every situation. The rest of us must struggle daily with the layers of illusion and misinformation that swirl around our conscious and subconscious minds. What is required here is nothing less than altering the very core of our entire beings. It isn't easy, but it is certainly worth the effort. The qualities associated with love are peace, health, serenity, and happiness. The qualities associated with not loving are war, disease, agitation, and misery. Can there be even a hint of doubt about which is the proper choice? We don't think so. All you need is love.

*A*ctions

▲ What are your most loving qualities? Allow yourself to reflect for a while each day on yourself as a loving person. Image yourself in real life difficult situations in which you act in a loving way.

▲ What are the obstacles within you that prevent you from being more loving? Focus on the most difficult one and imagine it each day having less power and control in your life.

▲ What sources of life help you to be a more loving person: unpressured time with loved ones, music, quiet time, nature, and the like? How can you have more of these experiences?

*A*lbum

Magical Mystery Tour; The Beatles; Parlophone CDP 7480622.

AND WHEN I DIE
▲ *(Nyro)* ▲

Blood, Sweat and Tears

*B*ackground

Songs about death deserve a category of their own in the history of American rock 'n' roll. "Teen Angel," "One Last Kiss," "Endless Sleep," "Ebony Eyes," "Honey," and a host of other hits all deal with teen tragedies and fatalities. "And When I Die," by the late Laura Nyro, was a little different. It took a look at death from a more mature and spiritual perspective. Her own recording of the song was only moderately successful. It wasn't until Blood, Sweat and Tears did a cover version on their multiplatinum second album that the song became part of the national consciousness. Released as a single in October of 1969, "And When I Die" climbed to number two on the charts.

*R*eflections

When you think about your own death, how do you feel? Are you terrified, somewhat fearful, curious, hopeful, expectant, or simply detached? Your response depends on how you answer two questions: Who is the God that I believe in? How do I feel about the way I've lived my life?

If you were brought up to envision God as a stern judge sitting up there with the big book open to your page, counting your good deeds and bad deeds, you are in serious trouble. No wonder you're scared to death of death. If you see God more as an all-loving father or mother figure, you are probably more prepared to die "naturally."

The second question is even more difficult to answer. Even if God is all loving and forgiving in general, will that apply to you? Will you be worthy? Will you make the grade? Suppose you try hard all your life but have just a few failures, or suppose you have done well except in one area: an addiction, an infidelity, or some tragic flaw like laziness or greed or lust. How will you be judged?

Part of our problem in dealing with these questions is not just religious, it is cultural. We live in a society of achievement. We are valued by what we accomplish, not just overall, but now, every day, again and again. We tend to be hard on ourselves, keeping account of our faults and disappointments. We transpose that mentality of society onto God. We believe that God will judge us the way we judge one another and the way we judge ourselves. That, of course, reduces God to the level of the small-minded or even vindictive creatures that we sometimes are, not the all-forgiving presence of unconditional love that we occasionally experience in one another.

*A*ctions

▲ Do you have a definition of God? Who or what is God for you? What kind of a relationship do you have with God?

▲ Do you believe in an afterlife? If so, what will it be like? Try to envision it.

▲ If you are extremely fearful of death, try to trace the cause of the fear back to your childhood. Did it come from your parents, teachers, clergy, family members, peers, or some other source?

▲ Have you read any of the literature about near-death experiences? The overwhelming story from those who seemed to have died or were even technically dead is of a very positive, loving presence. Read some of the literature.

*A*lbum

Blood, Sweat and Tears; Blood, Sweat and Tears; Columbia CK 9720.

BADLANDS
▲ *(Springsteen)* ▲
Bruce Springsteen

Background

When Bruce Springsteen first emerged from the swamps of Jersey in the early seventies, he was immediately tagged with the label the "New Dylan." This was an albatross that every promising singer-songwriter had to carry around for a while in the post-Dylan era of American music. It took a few albums for Bruce to find his own true voice as a recording artist, but it happened in dramatic fashion in 1975, with the release of *Born to Run*. This was followed three years later with another triumph—*Darkness on the Edge of Town*. The songs were edgier, moodier, but still laced with a defiant optimism best illustrated by the album's lead track, "Badlands."

Reflection

This is definitely one of the Springsteen anthems. It has the power to raise twenty thousand fans to their feet, screaming not only the chorus but the verses with a passion rarely heard even in the halls of rock 'n' roll. Why? At one time or other, every one of us has felt we were engulfed in some kind of "badlands," whether at work or in our personal lives. We can identify with Bruce's struggle to get out. We are challenged by his defiance that says "We'll keep pushing till it's understood and these badlands start treating us good." We are inspired by his belief in the power of love, his faith, and his hope in the face of great odds.

Springsteen has always appeared to his fans as "one of the guys," an outsider trying to make it. A part of Bruce still feels that way, despite his success, so when he belts out this song on stage it remains credible, with the intensity of a youth long since passed for him and perhaps half the audience.

If you were ever told by a parent, teacher, a coach, or a boss that you were a loser or an underachiever, or if you ever felt that way even if no one actually said it, then you can feel this song. If you still feel glad to be alive despite whatever badlands you are in, and you need a little support for those feelings, pop this one into your CD player. If you are still looking for that "one face that won't look through you," that will affirm who you are then sing along. If you have already found people like that you are truly fortunate. Invite them over to join you in singing one of rock's classic songs of hope.

*A*ctions

▲ Is there some badlands that you are presently in? What are the ways out that have worked for you in the past, the positive forces that have allowed you to face the badlands inside you and out? Go back to them now and get rejuvenated, whatever they are.

▲ All too often, when we are faced with a difficult problem or some form of depression, we become immobilized emotionally and even physically. If you find this is happening to you, for whatever reason, take inspiration from this song and take some positive steps, even just sharing your burden with a friend or doing something positive for yourself that may renew your strength and your hope.

▲ We know dozens of people who have used this song as a temporary remedy for a bad funk. If you know someone that you think this song might help, mention it.

*A*lbum

Darkness on the Edge of Town; Bruce Springsteen; Columbia CK 35318.

BLOWIN' IN THE WIND
▲ *(Dylan)* ▲

Bob Dylan

Background

"Blowin' in the Wind" is the song that started Bob Dylan on the journey from relative obscurity to superstardom. When he was signed to Columbia Records by John Hammond in 1962 and released his self-titled debut album, the scruffy, nasal singer was described in the hallways of his own record company as "Hammond's Folly." That all changed about a year later, when Peter, Paul, and Mary recorded a cover version of Dylan's "Blowin' in the Wind." The song immediately captured the imagination of the country and shot to number two on the charts. Suddenly, even Dylan's versions of his own songs began appearing regularly on the radio, and ultimately on the singles and album charts as well. But it was "Blowin' in the Wind" that sealed Dylan's reputation as a visionary. And no wonder . . .

Reflection

Throughout history every generation has had to deal with difficult, if not impossible, questions. The key is to do it in a way that is least destructive and actually accomplishes something. Bob Dylan, the preeminent musical poet of the sixties, captures the spirit of his generation's social questions about war and violence and racial injustice with a perception and a passion that are unparalleled in their power and eloquence. There is no easy answer however to his oft-repeated question, "How many times?" Answers are never given simplistically. They are out there somewhere, "blowin' in the wind," elusive to the grasp, yet temptingly near. In our society, we want quick answers and we want them now, if not sooner. Problems must be solved immediately. Pain must be relieved at once. Mysteries are fine for novels, but living in the mystery and seeking answers there rather than in a series of quick-fix solutions is too difficult for most people.

Poverty, injustice, and war have existed for every generation throughout history, and with them come deep, emotional, all-consuming questions. Dylan helped rally his generation to involvement in these issues and his songs, including this one, became anthems for the civil rights movement and the antiwar movement. These long, strife-ridden campaigns championed no easy answers. Through dedication and sacrifice, they helped to end racial segregation in America and played a major role in ending the most divisive conflict since the Civil War. Not bad for a bunch of outsiders who felt and expressed their beliefs, questions, and passions deeply.

*A*ctions

▲ What are the major social injustices that you see in our society today whose answers are "blowin' in the wind," apparent, yet seemingly beyond political solution? Do you feel strongly about any of these injustices?

▲ What are you doing to be a part of the solution? Do you try to learn more about the issues?

▲ If you are involved, do you feel you are making a difference? If not, what more can you do?

▲ Is there a personal injustice that you or a loved one suffered that seems unresolved, even though you feel there can be a just solution? Is there anything you can do to move toward a resolution? What resources do you need? What steps should you take?

*A*lbum

The Freewheelin' Bob Dylan; Bob Dylan; Columbia CK 8786.

BOTH SIDES NOW
▲ *(Mitchell)* ▲

Judy Collins

*B*ackground

She is the all-time queen of the confessional singer-songwriters—the role model, inspiration, and trailblazer for many of the female performers who have followed in her footsteps. Carole King, Carly Simon, and Laura Nyro deserve their due, but Joni Mitchell is in a class by herself. Albums such as *Ladies of the Canyon, Blue, For the Roses,* and *Court and Spark* are among the most successful and celebrated in music history, but many of us first discovered Joni through Judy Collins's sublime version of "Both Sides Now," which climbed to number eight on the U.S. charts in the fall of 1968.

*R*eflection

There are many sides to life, but you can also say that there are "both sides," an upside and a downside. There are times in your life when you manage to look at life from both sides, to see the positive and negative elements and choices before you make your decision. Most of the time, however, you look at life from one side, the positive or the negative, the proverbial half empty glass or the half full. Which is it for you?

Unfortunately, many of us too often look at life from a pessimistic, depressed, cynical, fearful insecurity. The glass is not just half empty, it is shattered. Where does that attitude come from? How can we fight it? The cause may be a series of tragedies, betrayals, and disappointments. These things do sometimes happen in a serial form, one after the other, with no let up and no relief in sight. It is enough to turn anyone sour. Let's face it, though, that's not usually the cause. It is more like a low-grade fever than an inferno in your body, more like a dull, deadening long-term pain than a pounding, excruciating headache. You live with it, but for long periods of your life you become disconnected with the other side of life, the upside. Somehow, a combination of genetics, your upbringing, and your present environment all combine to deal you a hand of downside cards. How can you play them or, better, how can you be dealt a new hand?

*A*ctions

▲ If you tend to look at life from the downside, allow yourself to be fully aware of what that means and what the consequences are for you and your relationships.

▲ What are the positive, upside elements in your life? How can you be more in touch with them, spend more time with them, and allow them to nourish you?

▲ Are there more upside experiences or attitudes that used to be a part of your life but have gotten lost along the way? Pick one that you really miss; an old friend, a physical activity, a lifegiving hobby, a spiritual practice or ritual, or just a lighter approach to life and focus on how you can reconnect with it.

▲ If you look at life from both sides, try to share your presence with a friend who is on the downside. If you are usually an upsider, be aware of all the rest of us who struggle with the downside throughout our lives.

*A*lbum

Wildflowers; Judy Collins; Elektra 74012-2.

BREAKING UP IS HARD TO DO

▲ (Sedaka/Greenfield) ▲

Neil Sedaka

Background

In the history of American top forty, only a few rare songs have been legitimate hits twice. "The Twist" by Chubby Checker was one; "Stand by Me" by Ben E. King was another (see page 170). One of the most interesting times this occurred involved the Neil Sedaka song "Breaking Up Is Hard to Do." It was a hit the first time in 1962, when Sedaka was racking up a string of teen-oriented top-forty hits. The original version was jaunty and upbeat, belying the sadness inherent in the song's lyrics. Thirteen years later, Sedaka rerecorded the song as a slower, sadder, world-weary ballad. Again, the message connected with record buyers and the new version reached number eight on the charts.

Reflection

Breaking up is hard to do for so many reasons. Suppose you are in a relationship that is dead or a living hell? There may be good reasons to stay in the relationship: you still have feelings for your partner, there are children involved, you made a commitment and you will honor it, you are afraid of change, and of hurting anyone, and on and on. Meanwhile, you are dying inside, little by little, day by day. You try all sorts of ways to numb the pain. You even go to counseling, alone or together. This is not some selfish whim. There is no cheap fling that has thrown you off the course of true love. You can honestly say you have tried. You know it's time to say goodbye, but you can't bring yourself to do it.

There are times in your life when you think breaking up will be relatively easy. The match is obviously off, the emotional investment is dwindling, and you're out of there, nice and clean with little damage done to either party. In your dreams! Damage is done, the pain is sometimes unbearable. Both the pain and the damage can be softened though, first by spending time getting in touch with your true feelings and, then, by speaking the truth with as much compassion and gentle strength that you can muster. Try to put yourself in your partner's shoes and understand the effects of the breakup on yourself as well as on him or her. Remember, you are experiencing the death of what was a live relationship, maybe even one that was a very good one for a long while. You need to mourn that death just as you would the physical death of a loved one. Depending on the length and intensity of the relationship, it may take you just as long to recover from this kind of death.

*A*ctions

▲ If you know you need to initiate a breakup because you have no other healthy choice, what is keeping you from doing it? How can you prepare so that you do the least damage, create the greatest good, and get on with your life? Instead of reacting in potentially dangerous anger or sulking, develop a plan for getting out.

▲ Now, for something completely different! Sometimes, when breaking up is hard to do it is precisely because you should not break up. Times may be hard, but there is still a solid basis for continuing the relationship. You may need to do some growing up, as may your partner. Counseling may be necessary. You may need to have a whole different attitude to each other or about specific problems within your relationship, but you can do it. Try to figure out ways to get back in, to strengthen the relationship. Keep trying until you break through, or until you know for certain that you've tried everything.

*A*lbum

All-Time Greatest Hits; Neil Sedaka; RCA 6876.

BRIDGE OVER TROUBLED WATER

▲ *(Simon)* ▲

Simon and Garfunkel

Background

"Bridge Over Troubled Water" is simply one of the most significant accomplishments of Paul Simon's long and distinguished career. The song (and the album from which it came) is one of the most successful, honored, and revered recordings of all time. Released in 1970, it was a number one single, a number-one album, a multiplatinum seller, and a multiple Grammy winner. The combination of Paul's brilliant writing and Art Garfunkel's angelic lead vocal propelled this song to the top of the American charts, where it remained for a solid six weeks. What chord did this tale of unconditional love and friendship touch in listeners the world over?

Reflection

A child dies, a husband abandons his wife and children, a fire or flood destroys a home and business, innocent bystanders are gunned down in a senseless drive-by shooting. These are only the most dramatic forms of troubled waters. Every one of us has troubled waters at one time or another in our lives—times when we truly feel so small and powerless that we wonder how we can even survive, no less pass through those raging waters. It is at those times that we need someone to be a bridge that helps us cross over into more peaceful and trouble-free times.

There are few more heartfelt, all-embracing outpourings of compassion in all of music than this pop hit. It is as though as we listen we are embraced in a blanket of love, a force so powerful that it can help overcome any combination of bad times that may have descended upon us. The sentiments in this song are worth meditating on over and over again, because they are at the heart of what it means to be truly human. First of all, to love someone so much that we will be at their side, to carry someone on your back because they cannot walk themselves, to be the bridge over troubled waters. But the reverse is also true—to be fully human also means to be willing to be carried for a while, to accept help, not to become permanently dependent but to regain true independence and interdependence.

These are the everyday stories of humanity at its very best, stories of the unsung heroes who are there to help their friends to be big again when they are feeling small.

Actions

▲ Remember a time when you were in troubled waters. Who was the bridge for you? Call to mind again how the person helped you. Try to visualize the face of the person who loved you through the crisis, and get in touch with your feelings for that person then and now.

▲ Have you been that bridge for someone in the past? How did it work out? Was the person grateful? How did you feel about it?

▲ Is there anyone who needs a bridge like that today? Are you willing to be that bridge?

▲ Listen to the song several times and feel the all-encompassing love that Simon and Garfunkel weave for you.

Album

Bridge Over Troubled Water; Simon and Garfunkel; Columbia CK 9914.

BRILLIANT DISGUISE
▲ *(Springsteen)* ▲

Bruce Springsteen

Background

When songwriters follow the time-honored advice to write about what they know, it leads to a sheaf of songs about themselves and their personal experiences. Of course, creativity, imagination, and vicarious experience are also powerful tools for the talented. But, every once in a while, a new album chronicles the very real life experiences of an artist in the throes of a crisis. *Rumours* by Fleetwood Mac certainly fits this category, as it unflinchingly dissects the crumbling relationships of the group's members at the height of their success. Similarly, Bruce Springsteen's 1987 release *Tunnel of Love* documents the deterioration of his first marriage. One of its most powerful songs is entitled "Brilliant Disguise."

Reflection

The very fact that many of us survive childhood in even reasonable wholeness is due, at least in part, to the brilliant disguise we develop for ourselves. We become the good boy, the dutiful daughter, the tough kid, the class clown, the brain, the superjock, and so on. It is not as though these disguises are phony or necessarily contradict who we really are, but they are limiting at best. There are many people who become their disguise and therefore never become full persons. Others develop new disguises as adults to meet challenging or difficult situations. We need to honor the gifts and opportunities that disguises gave us in childhood, then try to integrate them into our total personalities.

When you have two people in close relationship trying to work through their own disguises and see through each others' at the same time, the result can be the end of the relationship. However, it need not always end that way if you can gradually discover the wonderful people hiding within the disguises and the helpful qualities that are in the disguises themselves.

*A*ctions

▲ Did you play a particular role growing up in your family that called for a disguise? What was it? To what extent do you still have it? How is it now helpful or harmful to you?

▲ Recognize and respect how your disguise or role has helped you in your life so far, and then be honest about how it may now be limiting you or even haunting you. How can you bring a greater balance and whole-ness to your life by saying no to the demands of the disguise, and yes to other qualities or dimensions of your personality?

▲ If you were a good child, caretaker of a dysfunctional parent, or a re-sponsible, dedicated student, keep those wonderful qualities, but allow the other parts of you to emerge. Do not stay trapped in the image that others have of you which you have spent considerable time develop-ing. For example, if you have been a caretaker all your life, don't stop caring about other people but learn to take care of yourself as well.

*A*lbum

Tunnel of Love; Bruce Springsteen; Columbia CK 40999.

CAN'T BUY ME LOVE

▲ *(Lennon/McCartney)* ▲

The Beatles

*B*ackground

No question about it, 1964 was the year of the Beatles. From February 1st until May 8th, they controlled the number one position on the American charts with a string of hits that began with "I Want To Hold Your Hand" and ended with "Can't Buy Me Love." (Incidentally, it was "Hello Dolly" by Louis Armstrong that loosened the Beatles' rigid grip on the number-one slot.) "Can't Buy Me Love" was number one for five weeks and also ended up on the soundtrack of the Beatles first film, *A Hard Day's Night,* later that summer. The songwriting team of Lennon and McCartney could do no wrong, and was already displaying the kind of wit and sophistication that would make so many of their songs timeless.

*R*eflection

In an age of prenuptial agreements that detail how every dollar will be divided and near-royal wedding receptions that could feed the average American family for several years, this thirty-four-year-old Beatle song hearkens back to a more basic truth. When you truly love someone, you give all that you have, gifts beyond treasure, and you give them freely, joyfully. This generously mad approach to life is the antithesis of the extreme bottom-line mentality that Wall Street has promoted, especially during the last twenty years. This kind of love is the great social equalizer. The fat-cat multimillionaire may have dozens of the latest gadgets, luxurious houses, cars, and boats, and power. But what about love, trust, and friendship? Does anyone give him any of that freely or does he try to buy what you and I, no matter how poor we may be, offer and receive free?

Imagine: Love, the most important reality, can only be given freely. The same is true of trust and friendship and so many other precious gifts. Yet there is a price to pay for love—the price of responsibility, compassion, caring, and, sometimes, heroic service and sacrifice. It is truly a price that money can't pay, and those of us who are willing to pay the price receive rewards and gifts that will never be bankable.

*A*ctions

▲ What is the price you have paid for love throughout your life? Has it been worth it? Why?

▲ Have there been times when you were unwilling to pay the price, either because you thought it was too high or you just didn't have it in you? For example, taking care of a sick or infirm parent or child, supporting a spouse's career decision that involved great sacrifices for you, or supporting someone you love when that person makes a decision with which you strongly disagree. Do you regret your decisions now?

▲ Has anyone ever tried to buy your love? How? How did you react?

▲ Is there anyone to whom you want to give your love more freely? How can you take the first or the next step to do it?

*A*lbum

A Hard Day's Night; The Beatles; Parlophone CDP 7-46437 2.

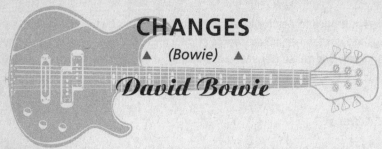

CHANGES
▲ *(Bowie)* ▲

David Bowie

Background

David Bowie is a true rock 'n' roll chameleon. He has gone through more stylistic changes than anyone else in popular music, with the possible exception of Neil Young. He began enjoying success in his native England in the mid- to late sixties. He had a rougher time of it in America. In 1969, "Space Oddity" received exposure on the more progressive FM stations in the states, but it was not until the release of *Hunky Dory* in 1971 that Bowie became a force on the American music scene. Interestingly, the song from that album which prefigured the many identities that Bowie would adopt in succeeding years was the one called "Changes."

Reflection

There was a man some years ago who was petrified of change. He knew there would be big changes in his job, and he agreed they were needed. Still, he could not wait until they were all in place and he had adjusted to them. Then he would have a new routine, a new set of daily certainties.

The point he never got was that change is a continuing reality in life. You can run from it, try to deny it, and, sometimes, even prevent it, but the possibility of change is always there, for better or worse. Some people never get used to change, others live in a frenetic series of ill-advised changes, but everyone must deal with changes throughout life.

If you have something positive, such as a good job or good relationship, you can live in fear that it will be taken away from you or that you will somehow blow it. Or, you can see life as a series of gifts that are not your possessions but which will be most fruitful when they are shared and celebrated and understood as evolving in your life. It is true that sometimes change brings loss. That is the most difficult change of all, because something that seemingly was yours and that you expected to last is lost. On the other hand, each change that you face brings the possibility of growth, healing, insight, and sometimes an opening to a previously undiscovered world of possibilities. It all depends on how you see it and how you act on it.

*A*ctions

▲ Do you consider yourself as someone who usually fears change or relishes it? Where do you think that part of your personality comes from?

▲ When you know a change is coming that you did not initiate, how do you prepare for it and cope with it?

▲ Are you willing to initiate needed change, or do you wait until you are forced to move?

▲   Choose a change you know is coming that you did not initiate. What is your plan to deal with it? What further resources do you need from within yourself and without?

▲ Choose a change that you want to make but do not know how, or are afraid to start. Try to envision the change successfully made. Now, begin to develop a critical path for making the change. When you feel ready, take the first step.

*A*lbum

Hunky Dory; David Bowie; RYKO RCD 10133.

CRAZY LOVE
▲ (Morrison) ▲
Van Morrison

*B*ackground

One of the most prolific and engaging artists of the last three decades has been the enigmatic Irish singer-songwriter Van Morrison. From his early recordings with the rock group Them, right up to the present moment, he has compiled a body of work comparable to the very best writers of his generation. Still, if one were forced to pick just one album from his vast catalog for that proverbial trip to a desert island, the consensus might just have to be his 1971 masterpiece, *Moondance*. It was a critical triumph as well as a huge commercial success, packed with amazing songs and performances such as the title track, "Caravan," "Into the Mystic," "Glad Tidings," and the one we've chosen—"Crazy Love."

*R*eflection

When two people fall in love there is often a kind of temporary madness that overcomes them. It allows them to overlook faults that others see, and to see wonders that others have never imagined. Without this crazy love the world would certainly be a less joyful and exciting place and, perhaps, the very continuation of the human race would be threatened. After all, it is while gazing in the eyes of the beloved that the desire to create a new life together begins.

A mother spends seemingly endless sleepless nights nursing a sick child. A soldier risks his life for a comrade fallen in battle. A spouse lovingly takes care of a dying partner day after day, long after the flames of passion have died and often without recognition. All of this is *agape,* unconditional love, crazy love, a love that the Greeks believed came from God. The love between two people newly in love is crazy in that it goes delightfully beyond the bounds of reason. Yet all these other experiences are crazy love as well, because they are selfless, they look for no return but to nourish and heal the person loved. It is the highest form of love, loving another in at least a shadow of the way that God loves.

*A*ctions

▲ Have you ever experienced any form of crazy love? Allow its power to re-enter you from time to time and experience the presence of the beloved once again.

▲ Crazy love can be a transforming experience. When you have loved and been loved that way you are never the same. Think about how crazy love has changed you for the better, and opened you up to a new dimension and depth of love.

▲ The seeming paradox here is that when you really try to love as uncondi-tionally as you can, the possibility of genuine acts of crazy love coming back to you increases. You don't just make a series of deals in which you give to get and love to be loved. You simply try to love without soci-ety's rules of "what's in it for me now, right now."

▲ If crazy love is in your life, cherish it, be thankful for it, and put it high-est on your list of priorities beyond priorities. There is no greater gift. Think of some joyful way of honoring that love and the person who shares it with you.

*A*lbum

Moondance; Van Morrison; Warner Bros. 3103-2.

CROSSROADS
▲ *(Johnson)* ▲
Cream

*B*ackground

Cream was one of the first so-called supergroups. Ginger Baker from the Graham Bond Organization and Jack Bruce from Manfred Mann joined forces with Yardbirds/John Mayall alumnus Eric Clapton to form the power trio in 1966. Together only two years, the group nonetheless produced a solid body of work including psychedelic originals and blues-rock interpretations. On their third album, *Wheels of Fire,* they finally got around to recording blues legend Robert Johnson's "Crossroads" which climbed to number twenty-eight on the American charts in 1969. The blues classic has since become a signature song for Clapton, and even served as the title of his four-CD boxed-set retrospective.

*R*eflections

There are only a few times in your life when you do certainly stand at the crossroads. It is not simply an important decision that you face. It is a life-determining, life-altering, or life-saving decision that effects the core of your being. Should you marry this person? Should you choose this career? How do you handle it? What to do first?

The first step is to make sure you know enough to make the decision—not just the pertinent facts but the feel or the fit of the situation for you. The second step is to evaluate the positives and negatives in your decision. Some people like to draw a line down the middle of a page and make two lists, which can be helpful in seeing all the items. Making lists often evokes responses that otherwise might remain buried in the recesses of your psyche, but it is not a precise formula. It calls for lengthy reflection, not spur of the moment decisions.

If you are still uncertain and know that your wellbeing is hanging in the balance, seek good advice or at least someone to listen to you as you spin out the options and your feelings about them. A good listener who asks a few well-placed questions can often help you see your choices in a different light. If you are very fortunate, you have at least one person in your life that you would trust with your life. That's the person you want to ask for advice, because the advice will come to you with love and also with a history of knowing you well.

After you have gone through this whole decisionmaking process with, perhaps, many further steps, try one more. Remove yourself from the process and do something entirely different that engages your energies for a while. Or simply be quiet, in prayer or meditation, and be attentive but relaxed. In time something will happen that may not solve your total crossroads dilemma but will take you forward.

*A*ctions

▲ If you are at a crossroads at this time in your life, try to remember another one, different though it may be. How did you get through it? Will what worked then still work now? What did you learn from the experience that you can apply now?

▲ If you feel that you failed miserably at a prior crossroads in your life, try to go back and get in touch with the elements that led to the mistake, so that they will not trap you again.

▲ Make sure you are in touch with your feelings as well as your intellect, as you prepare to make your big decisions and listen to that voice within you that is your guide, your center. Your final decision, as difficult and torturous as it may be, must come from your center for it to be genuine. Keep trying: It is a lifelong search for each of us.

*A*lbum

Crossroads; Eric Clapton; Polydor 835 261-2.

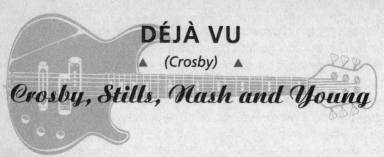

DÉJÀ VU
▲ (Crosby) ▲
Crosby, Stills, Nash and Young

Background

Literally translated from the French, it means "already seen." It is the most common form of psychic phenomena experienced and reported by average, everyday citizens around the globe. It is the very intense sensation that occurs when you walk into a room or find yourself in a certain situation and feel very strongly that, somehow, somewhere, you've already seen what you're seeing and done what you're doing. In 1970, when Crosby, Stills and Nash joined forces with Neil Young to produce an album of original material, they named the album after the David Crosby song "Déjà Vu." It soared to the top of the charts as the group began a summer tour but, by the end of the tour the group fell apart, only to regroup and breakup in different formations many times in the years ahead. Already seen, indeed!

Reflection

That great wordsmith Yogi Berra immortalized this French expression with his oft-quoted line "It's *déjà vu* all over again." The repetition of redundancy reigns but the point is well made.

Sometimes the experience of *déjà vu* is funny, other times it is eerily haunting, but there are times when it is downright annoying or even dangerous. You find yourself mindlessly making the same mistake again and again. You have some strange fascination with danger or a seductive attraction that keeps leading you to potentially destructive behavior. It not only seems like you've been here before, you have. A part of you says "Get me out of here," but there is another voice that says "Stick around, you're getting close to something great."

Real situations of *déjà vu* just happen and they are rare for most of us. These other situations are self-created *déjà vu*. At first, we may say "How did

I get into this situation again?" but a bit of self-reflection reveals a magnetic kind of attraction that leads us down the same road. The extreme of this is addiction, but there are many steps along the *déjà vu* spectrum, and not all of them are negative, by any means. There are those wonderful coincidences in which we find ourselves in the same delightful situations as before. Are they really coincidences or has some positive force within us or outside us drawn us there? Certainly, we need to be in enough control of our lives to keep us from the addiction dimension of *déjà vu,* but not so much so that we block out the wonders of *déjà vu.*

Actions

▲ You have probably had experiences of true *déjà vu* in which most of the elements of a situation line up as they did without any input from you. If they are good experiences, enjoy them, if they are scary, try not to make too much of them—unless the culprit behind these coincidences is you. You say to yourself "I've been here before. Here I am broke again, or out of a job again, or dumped again or in another bad relationship, or drunk and stoned again."

▲ The first step is obvious: Admit that you have a problem, that you are not really in control of your life.

▲ The second step is to seek help, perhaps from your network of family and friends, a counselor or a twelve-step group.

▲ The next step is to believe that you can change, that it does not have to be that way. Listen to the stories of others who faced similar problems and overcame them and finally remember situations from your past that you faced and overcame.

▲ When you have positive *déjà vu* experiences do you enjoy them? Do you learn anything from them?

Album

Déjà Vu; Crosby, Stills, Nash and Young; Atlantic SD 19118-2.

DID YOU EVER HAVE TO MAKE UP YOUR MIND?

▲ *(Sebastian)* ▲

The Lovin' Spoonful

Background

For a while in the midsixties, it looked as if America had been beaten at its own game. After inventing and nurturing rock 'n' roll through its formative years, we suddenly found ourselves playing second fiddle to Beatlemania and the British Invasion. Soon enough, though, the Colonies responded. Groups such as the Byrds, the Beach Boys, and Simon and Garfunkel began giving the Brits a run for their money. One of the most successful bands to emerge during this period was the New York–based Lovin' Spoonful. Led by singer-songwriter John Sebastian, the Spoonful in quick succession put ten good-time hits on the top forty charts. One of them, in May of 1966, asked the very interesting question "Did You Ever Have to Make Up Your Mind?"

Reflection

Sometimes decisionmaking is simple: choose A or B, say yes to one and no to the other. More often than not, in our society today, there are a variety of choices, not just chocolate or vanilla. In many ways, variety is the spice of life and most Americans delight in true freedom of choice whether it involves products, work, lifestyles, friends, belief systems, political candidates, or places to live. However, we do have to make up our minds dozens of times a day about moderately important items, and dozens of times in our lives about crucial life-effecting choices. Because of the mobility, education, and re-sources that many of us have, the need to choose has multiplied exponentially over the past century. How can we deal with this decisionmaking overload?

When I was fifteen years old I was walking down the street one day when suddenly it hit me. I had more than one choice about things. Some people were advising me to go one way on a certain issue, others were sug-gesting the opposite, and both were saying there were only two choices. I began to see that there were several other possible choices, and that I needed to see all of them and evaluate each in relation to the others. That insight was a big deal for a fifteen year old and it has always stayed with me. When I have to choose between one or the other I try to look hard to determine if these are my only choices.

Every choice has consequences. Being able to think through the consequences of very important choices and actually imagine them is an important step. The next step is to get beyond the thought process to the level of feelings and intuition. Sometimes the rational mind says one thing and the heart says another. The real question is what does the whole of you, the whole person, decide, despite all the the conflicting elements from outside and the conflicting emotions within? To answer that question you have not only to know the choices and consequences well but also know your own heart before you make up your mind.

Actions

▲ When you have an important decision to make it is important to employ both reflection and on-the-spot intuition. Sometimes, it just hits you and you know it's right. Usually, it is. Go with it. Other times, nothing definite strikes you and you need to know all the facts and consequences of your action, weigh the options, and take some time before you make your decision. It also helps if you have people you trust for advice. Often, if you hear yourself talking the problem through, you will detect something in your explanation that will influence your decision.

▲ When you are making the all-important decision that John Sebastian is singing about—to choose the right partner for life—be fully aware of why you are making your decision. Try to be as clear as possible about the negatives as well as the positives and be as sure as you can be about living with them.

Album

Anthology; The Lovin' Spoonful; Rhino R2 70944.

DON'T LET ME BE MISUNDERSTOOD

(Benjamin/Marcus/Caldwell) ▲

The Animals

*B*ackground

Eric Burdon and the Animals first achieved success in America with a number-one cover version of the traditional folk-blues song "House of the Rising Sun." They followed this with a string of hits that capitalized on the group's rough, working-class background, coupled with Burdon's black and blues-based vocals. "It's My Life," "We Gotta Get Out of This Place," and "I'm Crying," screamed out for better days and a better life seemingly just out of reach. The song that showed another side of the group, a more vulnerable side, was "Don't Let Me Be Misunderstood." Released in March 1965, it climbed to number fifteen on the American charts.

*R*eflection

Sometimes you never even know that it's happening while it's happening. At other times you know you are being misunderstood, but try as you might, you cannot set things straight. In either case, it is a terrible feeling. What is much worse is when the misunderstanding goes beyond a particular deed or series of words to your very person. No matter how much you protest, you have been misunderstood. You try to make it clearer. You start over again. You even apologize, but all to no avail. The other person has misunderstood you: your motives, your values, the core of your being.

You can usually clear up a misunderstanding if you work at it over a period of time. Sometimes, however, it is just not possible and you have to live with it, making sure that you do not allow it to take up more psychic space in your life than it deserves or than you can afford.

The most painful misunderstandings are with the people we love most. A bad misunderstanding can break a longstanding bond and go on for years, even a lifetime. There are many situations, though, in which time is a helpful healer. As time passes, passions decrease and an openness gradually emerges that seemed impossible before. The problem then may be that distances have developed and neither person knows how to take the first step back. The pain has been numbed, and fear of rejection or of opening old wounds has taken over the territory of the heart where understanding and love did once abide. Some people take misunderstandings to the grave, and often are driven to the grave by these same misunderstandings. Others begin a whole reawakening of a relationship by reaching out beyond the misunderstanding.

*A*ctions

▲ Minor misunderstandings can usually be avoided by being clear about your position and precise about your communication. Interestingly enough, the same rules hold true for most major misunderstandings. Get it right the first time.

▲ None of us gets it right all of the time. What do you do when you know you have been misunderstood? Try it again, more slowly. Put it in writing. Have someone else back you up and explain not only your true words but your good intentions.

▲ How do you deal with a long-term deep misunderstanding with an important person in your life? You did try again and again, a dozen different ways, without success. Don't give up, but don't beat yourself up. If you have tried your best, wait a while and then try again, but go on with your life.

*A*lbum

The Best of the Animals; The Animals; ABKCO 43242.

EASIER SAID THAN DONE
▲ *(Huff/Linton)* ▲

The Essex

Background

Rock 'n' roll music of the fifties and early sixties was very deceptive. It came out at a time when the genre was not taken very seriously as a form of expression. While its commercial potential was undeniable, the music itself was dismissed as primitive, simplistic, and eminently disposable. And some of it was. However, much of it touched deeper chords in its intended audience than anyone ever expected. Case in point, "Easier Said Than Done," by the Essex, their biggest hit and a number-one single, which came out in the summer of 1963. (Interesting footnote: The Essex got together while all the members were in the U.S. Marine Corps stationed in Okinawa. They had all their hits while in the service, and had to get permission from their superior officers to travel for promotional appearances and concerts.)

Reflection

You saw her standing with her friends at the dance. You were immediately attracted to her, but you never got up the guts to ask her to dance. You always wanted to go out with him. You saw him every day at work, you talked to him, and you knew he was available, but you never asked. You were going out for months. You knew you were falling in love, but you could not bring yourself to say the words "I love you." You have been married for many years and you rarely express the love that you still feel for your partner. You always intended to tell your mother, father, or grandparent how much you loved them but you have felt uncomfortable expressing your emotions. Tragically, the person you loved died before you could bring yourself to say how much love was in your heart. In every one of those situations, someone may have said to you, "Don't keep it to yourself, say it." Your reply may very well have been, "It's easier said than done."

That's the point of this thirty-five year old one-hit-wonder song. It is difficult for many of us to express our feelings of love on all levels. Why? The reasons may be buried deep in our personalities, in our upbringing, or in the customs of our society. Once we are aware of this reluctance, whatever its reasons, we can at least begin to figure out how we might express ourselves a little more openly. For some people, saying "I love you" and expressing affection come easy, but for some of us it's like having a root canal.

There is good news, though. Usually, once you begin to express your loving feelings in appropriate ways it gets easier and easier—easier said and easier done.

Actions

▲ In general, do you find it difficult to express affection to the people in your life, either verbally or physically? If you would really like to be able to communicate your feelings, start with the person with whom you feel most secure and begin in small ways to test the water.

▲ How do you accept affection or even compliments from others? Are you usually uncomfortable, doubting, or accepting?

▲ Are you all right in expressing affection most of the time except when it comes to the person you most love or want to love? What do you think is at the root of your reluctance? Try talking to a friend, family member, or counselor to get some advice on how to move forward. Don't continue to keep it all locked up inside.

Album

Billboard Top Rock 'n' Roll Hits—1963; Various Artists; Rhino R2 70624.

EMOTIONAL RESCUE

▲ *(Jagger/Richards)* ▲

The Rolling Stones

Background

The Rolling Stones are often described as the greatest rock 'n' roll band in the world and, at this point, few would dispute that they deserve the title. The sheer persistence and devotion to their craft that they have exhibited for thirty-five years puts them in a class by themselves. More than any other band, whatever the fad, whatever the trend, the Stones have thrived and survived and remained true to the blues-based origins which they so aspired to protect and preserve. This is not to say that they didn't experiment with different forms or sounds along the way. One such exploration resulted in the song "Emotional Rescue" which became a number-three single for the Stones at the height of the disco craze in 1980.

Reflection

Do you need an emotional rescue? The truth is, most of us do at one time or another, but it seems to go against the grain of good old American self-reliance. Just keep plugging away and you can beat it, whatever it is. Nonsense! We do need more self-reliance and less victimized wimpiness in our society, but each of us also needs understanding and compassion and, occasionally, an emotional rescue.

This does not necessarily call for an immediate visit to a therapist. A caring, insightful good listener-friend or family member can be the entire emotional-rescue team in some situations. You may just need someone to listen or give you a good piece of advice or reassuring embrace. Another part of the process for you simply can be to refocus, to step away from the emotional turmoil of your life, and go out and have a good time with friends, see a hilarious movie, become engaged in a deeply moving novel, play your favorite sport all out, retreat into nature and breathe in the beauties of creation, take an extended vacation, pray, or meditate. They can be escapes but, if properly used, they are healing experiences, a time to recreate the best in you and rediscover your center. Of course, there are times therapy is appropriate, especially when all else has failed or when you may feel isolated from family or friends.

You may need an emotional rescue after a traumatic experience like losing a job, a severe illness, a marital breakup, or the death of a loved one. Do not be ashamed! It happens to everyone. Seek help sooner rather then later before the difficulty reaches catastrophic proportions. If it does get that far, don't give up. Remember that it is possible to overcome emotional catastrophes—if you have the right kind of emotional rescue and if you are a willing partner in the rescue.

*A*ctions

▲ Reflect on the times when you needed an emotional rescue. How did you go about it? Who helped? Try to get in touch with your memories of the process, especially the successful parts and your feelings when you were past the crisis. This remembering is important because it can give you hope and encouragement for the next time you need an emotional rescue.

▲ Who and what are the parts of the emotional-rescue team for you? Just as your local fire department has a rescue team prepared for action, you need to know the sources of healing and rejuvenation for you when you become emotionally depleted or beyond that, emotionally threatened.

▲ Are you aware of the signs in your family and friends that say they need an emotional rescue? Are you willing to be part of their emotional-rescue team?

*A*lbum

Emotional Rescue; The Rolling Stones; Virgin 39523.

FATHER AND SON

▲ *(Stevens)* ▲

Background

Cat Stevens became a star in England in the mid-sixties. That early fame did not translate into instant success in America. It wasn't until a series of critically acclaimed and commercially popular albums in the early to midseventies that Stevens rose to the top of the pop heap in the States. *Tea for the Tillerman, Teaser and the Firecat,* and *Catch Bull at Four* are as good as anything his contemporaries were doing during the same period. In one of the oddest endings to a pop career ever, Stevens became a Muslim in 1979 and left the trappings of rock stardom far behind. Still, the best of his songs touched audiences then and now and left an indelible mark. "Father and Son" is certainly one of them.

Reflection

The father-child relationship is clearly one of the most significant in our lives. The man who plants the seed that results in our birth casts a long shadow over our entire existence. He's the link to our past and the guide to our future. A good father is a hero, pal, protector, and role model forever. A bad father leaves scars that often can't be healed in a lifetime. That's why the good ones are truly golden. Seen through a tiny child's eyes, they are infallible and invincible. One of the most gut-wrenching epiphanies that each one of us must face is the awareness that our parents are merely human, and capable of mistakes, weakness, and meanness. Worse yet is the inevitable realization that they are mortal and won't be with us forever.

It is easy to idealize the father-child relationship, but let's not forget the potential minefield that often stands between fathers and sons, daughters and fathers. Thickheadedness, generational differences, and coming of age passages can all lead to greater or lesser degrees of anger, misunderstanding, and conflict. Stubbornness and pride often get in the way of mending the relationship with one of the most important men, if not *the* most important man in our lives. We can think of nothing worse than permanent estrangement between fathers and children, nothing more haunting than unfinished business with a deceased parent.

To the extent that it is within your power, take the first step, make the first move. Pick up the phone, write it down in a letter, or drop by the house and say, "Dad, I love you." Often, it's the starting point for reconnecting a very important piece of our past and our future. And lest you think we are placing undue responsibility on the offspring, this advice works just as well in the opposite generational direction: "Son, I love you. Let's talk."

*A*ctions

▲ Do you or did you have a good relationship with your father? If so, how do you celebrate it (not just on Father's Day) and express your love and thankfulness to him? If not, what can you do to improve the relationship? Are you willing to take the first step even though you may still feel angry or hurt?

▲ If you were abused, either physically or emotionally, or in any combination, or if you were abandoned, have you confronted your father about it? Have you sought help in your own healing? What is the next step in the healing process?

▲ If you are a father or hope to become one, what does being a father mean to you? What are the qualities or gifts you want to give your child?

*A*lbum

Classics Volume 24; Cat Stevens; A&M CD 2522.

FEEL LIKE A NUMBER
▲ *(Seger)* ▲

Bob Seger and the Silver Bullet Band

Background

Bob Seger was another "overnight" sensation that, in reality, took a solid decade of hard work to come to fruition. Starting in the midsixties in his native Detroit, Seger enjoyed some regional success, and developed a rabid and loyal following, while never quite grabbing the brass ring of national pop stardom. Undaunted, he kept at it year after year, until the quality of his efforts could no longer be ignored. In 1976, the double album *Live Bullet* captured Bob's incredible live performance. Later that year, the exquisitely crafted studio album *Night Moves* catapulted Bob Seger and the Silver Bullet Band to the heights of rock stardom. They followed it up with *Stranger in Town,* an equally impressive album full of working-class anthems, such as the very emotional and powerful "Feel Like a Number."

Reflection

With the IRS you certainly are just a number, and that's all right, as long as they don't call your number. If you feel that way at work, however, you have a problem.

Bob Seger paints a powerful picture in this song of a man trapped in the impersonality of our mass society, someone who feels like a mere number, a small speck in a vast anonymous universe. No one values him for who he is. He is a man unrecognized and unappreciated.

Each one of us has a story inside that we need to tell. If no one will listen, we get sick and a little piece of us dies. A major part of that story is our creativity and our desire to use it to make our mark, to make a difference in the world. That is true not only for the financial, artistic, scientific, and other superstars of society; it is true for all of us. Some of us have obvious talents which we are paid well to display. Some of us struggle for recognition, or worse, do not even recognize our own creativity.

We are not numbers. We are not cogs on a wheel despite what society or our employers or schools try to make us feel. Each of us, by the very fact of our humanity, is distinct and has something inside that can make a special contribution to all.

*A*ctions

▲ Do you feel like a mere number at work or have you found your place, your passion? If not, what are your options: another job, another career, a second career while keeping the day job for survival?

▲ How about exercising your creativity in volunteering or in a hobby? Remember, your talent need not necessarily be your livelihood. It is wonderful when someone actually pays you to live your dream, but you don't need to be paid for your creativity to be authentic and appreciated.

▲ Ask yourself what makes you special, more than a number, and how you can develop those parts of you that help you to feel truly alive and good about yourself.

*A*lbum

Stranger in Town; Bob Seger; Capitol SW 11698.

FOREVER YOUNG

▲ *(Dylan)* ▲

Bob Dylan

Background

In 1974, Bob Dylan took a gamble. He left his long-time label, Columbia, for Asylum Records, a new company formed by media mogul David Geffen. The detour turned out to be short-lived. Dylan returned to the fold at Columbia just a couple of years later, but the music he produced at Asylum easily equaled the high standard he has maintained for himself throughout his nearly four-decade career. Songs such as "On a Night Like This" and "You Angel You," fit very nicely into the Dylan catalog, but one track on the *Planet Waves* album split from the pack to become an all-time Dylan classic. That song is "Forever Young," and, like many of the titles in this volume, it can easily be read as a prayer.

Reflection

John Hammond was my friend. He was also one of the most dynamic, life-filled people I ever met. He discovered Count Basie, Billie Holiday, Aretha Franklin, Bob Dylan, and Bruce Springsteen, among others. He was always excited about music and politics and almost anything else of importance. He took delight in the creativity of others and used his own creativity and substantial resources to help them make their mark. John stayed forever young.

At his memorial service, Bruce Springsteen stepped forward and sang "Forever Young," and tears came to my eyes. Bruce had quite obviously experienced this powerful force deep inside his friend and mentor that never faded until John faded into death.

You can often see this quality of aliveness and wonder in small children . Usually it is gone by the preteen years, slowly squeezed out by thousands of warnings and criticisms and complaints from well-meaning parents and teachers. It resurfaces for a while when you fall in love or have a child of your own or become involved in some exciting creative adventure, but there are always forces within you and without that fight against it, that try to capture it again, discourage it, put it back in the bottle lest its power cause ripples that might disturb.

*A*ctions

▲ What are the forces that keep you from being forever young in your spirit? Name them, expose them, write them down so that you may know them, and begin to challenge the power they have over you.

▲ What are the qualities in you that can keep you forever young? Is it your desire for knowledge, adventure, or creativity?

▲ How about your sense of humor or sensitivity to people? How can you unleash those forces of life, and let them play a little?

▲ Do at least one thing for yourself every day that helps you to be forever young.

*A*lbum

Planet Waves; Bob Dylan; Columbia CK 37637.

GET TOGETHER
▲ *(Powers)* ▲

The Youngbloods

Background

All right, here's the story and it's a good one. In the mid-sixties, songwriter Dino Valenti, using the pseudonym Chet Powers, wrote the ultimate brotherhood anthem "Get Together." The song was recorded by the Jefferson Airplane and the Chad Mitchell Trio, among others, but the definitive version was done by good time folk-rockers the Youngbloods. It was released as a single in 1967 and enjoyed some regional success but failed to chart nationally. End of story, right? Wrong! In 1969, the song was used as the background music for a public service announcement about brotherhood aimed at music radio stations. Listeners called in asking for information about the record. RCA rereleased the single in the summer of '69, and it climbed to number five on the national charts. We told you it was a good story.

Reflection

When people talk about the sixties, they are probably not referring to the actual chronological decade that began on January 1, 1960 and ended on December 31, 1969. They are more likely referring to that tumultuous period in American and world history during which a great number of cataclysmic events took place. Using those events as our measure or guideline, a much more accurate time frame for the sixties might be November 22, 1963 to August 9, 1974—the assassination of John F. Kennedy to the resignation of Richard M. Nixon. Those two presidential milestones serve as the bookends that encompassed such disparate events as the Vietnam War, the murders of Martin Luther King, Jr. and Robert Kennedy, the first man to walk on the moon, and Watergate.

What a decade! The rhetoric was loud and jarring. The passions were heartfelt and overflowing, and the divisions were as deep and real as anything America had experienced since the Civil War. Nonetheless, there was also hope and optimism in large abundance, expressed most notably in the music of the period. Millions of young people turned instinctively to the folk-and-rock music of the sixties to cure the ills, solve the problems, and heal the rifts that separated young and old, hawk and dove, and black and white.

"Get Together" was one of the great proclamations of this attitude but, somehow, as the years went by, it became stereotyped as hippie hogwash, an antiquated ode to the excesses of the peace and love generation. But, let's take another look and listen. There's nothing antiquated about the message of this song at all. Over thirty years later, it still speaks pointedly and elo-quently about the physical, spiritual, emotional and biological need of all liv-ing creatures to express and receive love. If we fail to live up to those ideals, it's not the song's fault. . . . it's ours!

$\mathcal{A}$ctions

▲ Millions of Americans live in cities and suburbs, clothed in self-created anonymity, invisible to neighbors and their larger community. Have you dropped out, become a loner, or become too busy to be involved in much of anything beyond yourself, your job, and your immediate family?

▲ Make a list of your community involvements (church or temple, school, civic association, political or social clubs, etc). It may be a very short list. Is there something you would like to join or volunteer for? How can you find the time? How do you make the move?

▲ Is there some issue or cause that you care about but feel powerless to in-fluence? Take the advice of this song and get together with an effec-tive group with whom you can share your voice.

$\mathcal{A}$lbum

Best of the Youngbloods; The Youngbloods; RCA 3280-2-R.

GIVE A DAMN

▲ *(Scharf/Dorough)* ▲

Spanky and Our Gang

Background

Spanky and Our Gang may be the most unlikely group to appear in this book. Known primarily for their soaring five-part harmonies and frothy pop-rock confections, they placed five songs in the American Top forty in 1967 and 1968, before coming apart at the end of the decade after the death of one of the group members and a parting of the ways for the others. It is their more lighthearted material that still gets played on the oldies stations, such as "Lazy Day" and "Sunday Will Never Be the Same." Still, the song that struck a chord with us is one of the last things they recorded together. It was called "Give A Damn" and, like one of the other songs in this book, it was used as background music for a public-service radio spot promoting the Urban League. By popular demand, it was released as a single, and its plainspoken, activist message hit home with American record buyers.

Reflection

If there is any song in our book that is a period piece, this is it. Nineteen sixty-eight was perhaps the most tumultuous year in postwar America: the Vietnam War, civil rights and antiwar protests, the Democratic National Convention, urban riots, the sexual revolution in full swing, and a growing awareness of the reality of inequalities and injustice in our society. It was an age in which we were challenged to give a damn about society, about the neighborhood, about people beyond our immediate families and friends. It was also an age of youthful optimism. We believed we could change the world. We believed we could make a difference. We believed in the power of government to do good as well as evil and we—or at least some of us— challenged the government in the halls of congress, in the courts, in the media, and on the streets to serve the needs and rights of all the people, not just the powerful.

Some of us are still fighting these battles thirty years later, but we believe that successful change in the nineties will come most often through the work of the thousands of community-based groups that have sprung up all over the country during the last fifteen years. They do not just provide emergency food and shelter but help people to become self-reliant through education, job training, community economic development, and programs to provide housing, healthcare, childcare, and other services that focus on people's strengths. When you join such a group, you will give a damn with a whole new power even beyond what Spanky was singing about in that troubling yet exciting decade. It is fast becoming near ancient history but it left us a great unmet challenge and a renewed energy to meet that challenge.

*A*ctions

▲ To what extent have you been infected with the great media hype of our society (and many others) that says "get yours first," "beat out the other guy or gal," "let them take care of themselves," or "no good deed goes unpunished." Be honest, now!

▲ How do you show that you give a damn beyond yourself and your family? Do you give of your time and your resources? How? Where? Why? Do you feel guilty if you don't? Is it social pressure, or, do you really feel good about giving? Have you found that when you volunteer or just do a good deed on your own, that you feel good about yourself, whether you get praised or not?

*A*lbum

Greatest Hits; Spanky and Our Gang; Mercury 832 584-2.

GIVE ME SOME TRUTH

▲ *(Lennon)* ▲

John Lennon

Background

In the aftermath of the dissolution of the Beatles, each band member spent the first postbreakup year reclaiming his individual identity. John Lennon went through this process the most visibly, the most vocally, and the most publicly. From his bed-ins for peace with Yoko and his spill-your-guts interviews in the rock press, John was determined to peel away all the layers of glory and stardom that had accumulated around him, and strip down (literally and figuratively!) to the basic core truth about himself as he perceived it. He dabbled in various kinds of therapy including one called Arthur Janov's Primal Scream Therapy. These experiences overflowed into his music and can be heard being practiced on early solo tracks such as "God" and "Mother." One of the best of these songs is "Give Me Some Truth" from the *Imagine* album.

Reflections

If you ask someone for the correct time or which track your train is on, you expect a truthful answer. Anything less could cause you, at least, inconvenience and, perhaps, disaster. On a much deeper level, if you reveal the secrets of your heart to a trusted friend, you expect that person to respect your privacy. If the friend blabs the intimate details of your story to anyone else and you find out, you will most probably feel that your trust has been betrayed and your friendship shaken or even destroyed.

There are certain situations, though, in which telling the truth is not so simple. If a good friend asks your opinion about how she looks or how well he did a particular task you may wonder just how much truth you should include in your answer. The best guideline for these difficult truth-challenging situations is to remember that truth is not simply a self-enclosed reality. It often exists within the context of a relationship. The answer to the question of what time it is consists of objective information—four o'clock, or six-thirty. The answer to "How do I look?" is more complex, because feelings, self-esteem, and the future of a relationship are all involved. So, when people ask you a question and you know you must give them some truth, ask yourself just how much they really want and can handle, and remember always to speak the truth with love and understanding. That can make a difficult truth heard rather than resisted.

*A*ctions

▲ Do you consider yourself a truthful person? If not, what are you doing to be more truthful? The first step may be to discover why you lie or evade and distort the truth. Try to find a pattern or ask someone you trust who knows your problem to give you some insight about how the pattern works.

▲ Are there people in your life who have a problem with truth, either in telling the truth or admitting the truth about themselves or a particular situation or person? How far do you let the problem go before confronting it? The tough part is what to do, what to say, and how to say it. The clue is that if you know that the lack of truthfulness is hurting a friend or the people around that friend, someone must do something. Are you the right someone?

*A*lbum

Imagine; John Lennon; Parlophone CDP 7 46641 2.

GLORY DAYS
▲ *(Springsteen)* ▲
Bruce Springsteen

Background

Bruce Springsteen's ascension to the peak of rock stardom occurred in several stages. First came the terrific reviews and rabidly positive word of mouth from fans and journalists alike. Then came the roaring success of *Born to Run,* and the simultaneous covers of *Time* and *Newsweek* in 1975. Legal problems and artistic soul-searching put things on hold for a while, but in 1984 all the elements came together to launch Bruce Springsteen and the E Street Band to the pinnacle of international stardom. The album was titled *Born in the U.S.A.,* and seven of its songs made it to the top ten on the singles charts. One of the best, that captured the groups' camaraderie and self-deprecating humor, was "Glory Days."

Reflection

When you are a teenage beauty or superjock or brain, you may have already tasted some glory and you may believe it will never end. Why not? You're on top of the world and the future looks boundless. Let's go a step further beyond the song, and imagine the lives of all those Wall Street wonders, sports stars, and supermodels. They make the first million before they hit thirty, maybe several million. What next? They, too, may end up trapped in their own boring stories.

Real glory comes from the quality and fidelity of your relationships to your family, friends, and partners, the continuing exercise of your creativity, whatever it is, and your service to the community. Does that sound hopelessly old-fashioned in this age of instant fame and fortune? Maybe so, but millions of average people find glory and even happiness far from the momentary spotlight of stardom and the elusive security of megabucks. They have their glory days now in the privacy of their own lives.

Most of us have stories of past glories and they are an important part of who we are. The stories are not boring in themselves as occasional reminiscences. They are beyond boring when they become obsessions that fill an otherwise empty life, whether from former superstars now considered has-beens, or the local high-school celebs of Bruce Springsteen's amazingly real cast of characters.

Whether we realize it or not, we have had many glory days: the birth of a child, a quiet walk on the beach with the person we love, the day we graduated, landed that long sought-after job or promotion, a time of reconciliation with an alienated relative or friend, a difficult decision successfully made, a spiritual experience of wonder and feeling loved, or perhaps a time of profound thankfulness for being alive and for all we have been given. These are the glory days.

*A*ctions

▲ Try to recall five glory days in your life. They may now be faded or fractured by broken relationships or broken dreams, but they were there. They had a power. Try to get in touch with that energy. What made those days glorious?

▲ Where is the glory in your life now? Are you aware of it, in touch with it, or is it passing you by? What can you do to reclaim the glory that is yours and enjoy it? Maybe it is spending more time with the people you love the most or doing what you really like to do or allowing yourself to experience life in a whole new dimension you have never tried, engaging parts of you that have never been in play. Maybe it is seeing what is instead of what could have been.

*A*lbum

Born in the USA; Bruce Springsteen; Columbia CK 38653.

GOD ONLY KNOWS
▲ *(Wilson/Asher)* ▲
The Beach Boys

Background

There was a famous magazine article written about Brian Wilson in the mid-sixties entitled "Goodbye Surfing, Hello God." All these years later, those four words still pretty neatly sum up the amazing transformation that Wilson underwent as the leader of one of America's most successful rock 'n' roll groups ever—the Beach Boys. From 1962 to 1965, the Beach Boys epitomized the burgeoning California culture and lifestyle. Surfing, cars, and California girls provided the subject matter for an infinite number of Beach Boys classics. But then, beset by personal problems and drug-related psychological illness, Wilson ceased performing live and concentrated instead on producing a new studio masterpiece. Despite the pressures and problems, he did it. *Pet Sounds* is one of the greatest and most satisfying albums in rock 'n' roll history. One of its many standout tracks is "God Only Knows."

Reflection

It is true that God only knows how much anyone of us loves anyone else, but there are ways of showing love that all too often get lost in the busy-ness of everyday life or the dark recesses of our own insecurity.

Let's start with hugs. Remember that billboard some years back that said "Have you hugged your kids today?" Children need hugs, but so do adults. A recent study says that a person needs at least two hugs a day to feel somewhat emotionally healthy. Four is the average and eight can make a major difference in turning a moderately depressed person into a happier, functioning person.

Telling people we love them and then backing up the words with deeds should be a normal part of our everyday life. However, days and weeks can go by without the awareness that we are not sharing the signs and the reality of love with the very people we love most. Routine sets in; other demands keep us busy. Resentments build up, a dozen real and imagined personal slights are perceived to be more serious than they are and, gradually, distances develop. We wake up one day on different emotional shores, having drifted apart from the people we love most. Signs of affection, acts of kindness, and words of caring all act as anchors that keep us connected with our emotional home port. They allow us to endure the worst of storms that are part of everyone's experiences.

*A*ctions

▲ Whether you are aware of it or not, you want and need affection and kindness—everyone does. Do you find it difficult to express affection, physically or verbally?

▲ Do you receive affection well, in the forms of hugs of kisses? Are you able to tell the people you love that you love them and care about them? Do you do it often enough? If the answer to these questions is no, what can you do about it?

▲ Start by complimenting and thanking your family and friends more, not to the point of silliness but appropriately.

▲ When someone offers you compliments and thanks in return, accept them graciously.

▲ Begin to offer appropriate (that all-important word again) signs of physical and verbal affection more often, and rejoice when they are accepted well and when they are returned to you. Most important, believe that you are worthy of being appreciated and loved.

*A*lbums

Pet Sounds; The Beach Boys; Capitol CDP 7 484212.

HAVEN'T GOT TIME FOR THE PAIN

▲ *(Simon/Brackman)* ▲

Carly Simon

*B*ackground

"That's the Way I've Always Heard It Should Be" was Carly Simon's first solo hit in 1971. The album it came from set the tone and established the formula for a series of successful recordings at the height of the confessional singer-songwriter phenomenon in America. Love, sex, and relationships were the major themes of Carly's songs throughout this period. Many of them resonated with a mass audience, which put Carly on the singles charts eleven times between 1971 and 1980. "Haven't Got Time for the Pain" from the *Hotcakes* album was her fifth solo hit, peaking at number fourteen on the charts in the summer of 1974. While it was successfully used as the music for a headache remedy commercial, we're pretty certain that's not the kind of pain she was talking about!

*R*eflection

It is strange how certain kinds of suffering, especially the bittersweet suffering that comes from losing a love, can become the sustenance of self-absorption. Each moment is relived despite, or maybe because of, the pain it will re-create. Depression has cut so deeply that it can truly be said that the suffering of loss and longing is the most vibrant force in life.

In this song, the answer to the pain is simple. A wonderful new person enters her life and the pain is magically gone because there is so much joy, so much love. There is literally no time for the pain nor is there a reason any longer. In real life, this sometimes happens. Great! But what about all those times when there is no one offering such a complete pain reliever?

There are two roads to travel here, but usually neither is enough by itself. You might try throwing yourself into endless activity to get out of the depression and stop focussing on the pain. You might also try to confront the source of the pain itself through counseling, prayer, meditation, or conversations with helpful, loyal friends. All of these steps are appropriate for healing, but it is the combination that is most effective. Activity to get your mind off yourself and your pain is very healthy, if you are not simply using it to avoid coming to grips with the loss or hurt. Getting to the source of the problem is also important, but make sure you don't wallow in the pain and let it become a kind of narcotic, entrapping you and taking away your power to act. The combination of reflection and action is usually the best pain reliever. And, it is the best way to prepare yourself for that "white light" of love that will eventually come from a person who can be your true lover.

Actions

▲ Try to remember a painful situation from the past that is no longer a problem. How did you work through it? What steps did you take? What and who was most helpful to you?

▲ Is there a great suffering in your life now to which you can apply any of those lessons?

▲ Have you or someone you know become self-absorbed in pain? What was the result? What was the way out?

Album

Hotcakes; Carly Simon; Elektra 1002-2.

HE AIN'T HEAVY, HE'S MY BROTHER
▲ *(Scott/Russell)* ▲

The Hollies

Background

It was a famous expression long before it made the charts by the Hollies in 1970. I can still see the illustration on Christmas seals soliciting funds for Boys Town, the home for troubled boys started by Father Flanagan and immortalized in the motion picture starring Spencer Tracy. The original image on the stamp always struck me as quite literal: The illustration showed a young boy carrying his younger brother in his arms. Composers B. Scott and B. Russell used the phrase as a metaphor to get across the bigger notion that all men are brothers. This anthem for brotherhood touched the hearts of record buyers and became the Hollies' first top-forty hit in four years. By the way, forgive the language of thirty years ago: It works just as well as "She Ain't Heavy, She's My Sister."

Reflection

Am I my brother's keeper? This age-old biblical question sends powerful reverberations thundering throughout society, through the halls of government, the boardrooms of industry, the tens of thousands of nonprofit social service agencies, and into the conscience of each of us. Or does it? The dominant ethic or lack of ethic in many of our institutions, if not in our minds and hearts, is "Get yours first," "Beat out the other guy," "Don't help them, they're lazy or stupid or _____." Fill in the blank with whatever is your prejudice of choice.

This song, which comes from an age of great social activism, responds directly and positively to the biblical question: Who is my brother or sister? If you accept the ancient Judeo-Christian position that we are all brothers and sisters, children of the same God, then the answer is real. The burden becomes lighter because the relationship is perceived differently.

Suppose, though, that your "brother" is an irresponsible drug addict or alcoholic, or a mean, grumpy old man who abused you in your childhood. Suppose your "sister" is a senile, old lady who emotionally abandoned you as a child or the love of your life who ran off with another person and is now alone again, impoverished and asking for your help. Are you that person's keeper? The answer resounds clearly throughout the ages. Yes! It is not necessarily a comforting answer. It is a responsibility, but not usually a call to take over someone's life and give up your own. There are heroic examples of that, but usually the best route is to provide support and challenge and, at the same time, a love that empowers, that gives hope but does not take over someone's life. The support and challenge may be accepted as a true gift by the person in need or it might be rejected again and again. The question then becomes, how often do I try? How long do I remain? The answer depends upon how long you can maintain hope and perseverance and how strongly you believe the title of this song.

$\mathcal{A}$ctions

▲ Is there someone who is a heavy burden in your life, either physically, financially, emotionally, or in any other way? How do you feel about the burden? Is it dragging you down, or is it lightened by the way you approach it? What can you do to lessen the burden while still helping the person?

▲ Is there someone that you know you should help, but for some reason you haven't? Can you face that responsibility without it becoming debilitating?

▲ Are you in a situation in which your help is doing more harm than good, perhaps disempowering the person? How can you change that?

▲ Has someone recently helped you bear your burdens? How have you responded? Have you been thankful or resentful? How have you expressed your feelings? Do you feel good about the relationship?

$\mathcal{A}$lbum

Anthology; The Hollies; Epic EGK 46161.

HELP ME MAKE IT THROUGH THE NIGHT

▲ *(Kristofferson)* ▲

Kris Kristofferson

*B*ackground

Kris Kristofferson was one of the unlikeliest pop stars of the seventies. Most of his experiences earlier in life pointed him in the direction of more intellectual pursuits. He received a Ph.D. from Pomona College in the late fifties, and went to Oxford University in England as a Rhodes Scholar. After a stint in the army, he was offered a teaching position at West Point, where he thought he might try his hand at writing the great American novel. He also possessed a gift for songwriting which kept tugging at him as well. A meeting with his hero, country legend Johnny Cash, convinced him to try songwriting full-time. He moved to Nashville, and worked as a janitor at the Columbia recording studio. (He was on the job while Bob Dylan was recording *Blonde on Blonde* in 1966.) Soon after, his songs were being recorded by the biggest names in country and rock, and he was offered the chance to record his own songs on Monument Records. That first album contained a number of Kristofferson classics, including "Sunday Morning Coming Down," "Me and Bobby McGee," and "Help Me Make It Through the Night."

*R*eflection

Nighttime is fright time. If you can help someone make it through the night you may well have saved a life. Imagine that! You spend a few hours of your life, pressured and harrowing though they may be, and you have helped save someone's life, most probably someone that you care about deeply. That person needed you to get over the hump, past the terrors of the night, and you were there. This does not mean that the problems go away in the morning, but they may look radically different in the light of day, and you may persuade your friend to seek lasting help.

Think about the troubled nights that you have spent alone. This song title may have become your prayer, and that prayer may have helped get you through. You were facing a difficult decision or confrontation and the long, tortured night gave you the words and the attitude you needed. You were awaiting possible good or bad news that could change your life, and the struggles of the night allowed you to think through the implications of the news and begin to develop a plan to make the best of it, one way or the other. There are good lessons to be learned and strength to be drawn from these hard nights. Sometimes, though, it would be wonderful to have someone there to hold you and comfort you all through the night.

Actions

▲ What do you do when you are having a tough night? The first step is to identify the cause of the trouble. If it is physical pain or emotional anxiety, the solutions lie in medication or relaxation techniques. If the problem is connected with ongoing events in your life, try to make the time an opportunity to gain insight by allowing yourself to struggle on a deeper level than you ordinarily would during the day.

▲ If you suspect you have a sleeping disorder, don't let it ruin your life. Get help! It doesn't have to go on that way.

▲ Losing a night's sleep is not something anyone enjoys. Losing the life of someone you care about is on a whole other level. Try to listen with your third ear, the one connected directly to your heart, when someone asks you for help through a potentially perilous night. You may lose some sleep, but save a life.

Albums

Songs of Kristofferson; Kris Kristofferson; Monument AK 44350.

HELP!
▲ (Lennon/McCartney) ▲
The Beatles

Background

Impossible as it seems, Beatlemania intensified in 1965. The whole phenomenon escalated to higher and higher levels, all at breakneck speed: more
back-to-back number-one singles, ever increasingly adventurous albums,
more live appearances that moved from concert halls to sports stadiums.
And, in the midst of all this, a second full-length motion picture (this one in
color) to follow up their dazzlingly successful debut, *A Hard Day's Night*. The
working title for the new film was *Eight Arms to Hold You*, but that was
changed to *Help!* after the John Lennon song, which became yet another
number-one single. It wasn't until a few years later that we realized that the
song was literally John's shout for help, a plea for some relief from the un-
ending demands of the crazy success that engulfed his life.

Reflection

This song is more than a cry for help; it is a relentless plea of desperation from
someone who has become detached from all of his life's securities. Self-as-
surance, which was present in the past, has departed, for whatever reasons,
and the protagonist is in a deep funk, seeking help from anyone. Sound familiar?

Undoubtedly, you have heard these pleas from people you love more
than once in your life, and have also made them yourself. There are several
apt phrases that describe the situation: "I'm at the end of my rope," "I've
lost it," "I have no place to turn." There is a whole combination of feelings
here, but the most apparent are powerlessness and isolation. Interestingly,
getting at those two feelings and working through them are the keys to the
help you need.

Are you really powerless, or do you only feel that way? Most of the time you are not totally powerless, but you may seem to be in a particular part of your life. Get back in touch with the power you do have and are expressing, no matter how small it may seem to you. Work with what you have, and build on it. At each step, feel the power at work; do not focus on the power you do not yet have.

Isolation goes hand-in-hand with powerlessness. When you break through the isolation and become reconnected with people who can give you a different perspective on your seeming powerlessness, you begin to have a chance to break out of your desperation. This is not the whole cure to the malady: You still have a long way to go, but it's not a bad first step.

*A*ctions

▲ If you are feeling desperate, try to trace the source(s) of the feeling. Does it come from events completely beyond your control, or did you play a role in abdicating your own power? If so, try to reconstruct how you let it slip away. Did someone overpower you with strength, or eat away at your strength with their everpresent, demanding weaknesses? Sometimes fighting weakness is harder than battling strength, but when you know what is going on, you at least have a chance. Whatever the source of your desperation and powerlessness, begin a step-by-step plan to come back to a healthy sense of power. Begin by tapping into the power that is within you, then look beyond your own capabilities and ask for outside help.

▲ If there is someone in your life who needs assistance, consider what is appropriate for you to do that will be helpful without creating undo dependency. Then, reach into your heart and touch that well of compassion that you may not know is there.

*A*lbum

Help!; The Beatles; Parlophone CDP 7 46439 2.

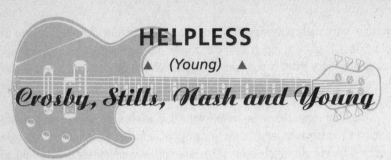

HELPLESS
▲ *(Young)* ▲

Crosby, Stills, Nash and Young

Background

The 1969 debut album by Crosby, Stills and Nash could not have been more successful; it immediately established the trio as a dominant force in rock 'n' roll. Nonetheless, when it came time to go out on the road, the group felt it needed some extra punch. They turned to Stephen Stills's former partner in the Buffalo Springfield, Neil Young. The results were electrifying indeed. The new quartet made a good thing even better. After a maiden tour that included their legendary appearance at Woodstock, the foursome headed into the studio to produce a second album. The result was *Déjà Vu,* released in March 1970. Though his tenure with CSNY was short-lived, Young's contributions enhanced the group's stature and added a couple of instantly memorable offerings to their repertoire, including the largely autobiographical "Helpless."

Reflection

When is someone truly helpless? When that person is completely paralyzed, lives on a respirator, and is fed intravenously? No! There are extraordinary stories of people fighting back step-by-step to some semblance of full human life. The real question is how to help people who need assistance without encouraging dependence.

We suggest a concept called *supportive challenge.* In most situations of need, people are offered either support or challenge, but rarely both. The typical hardass approach says "Get off your rear end and just do it. If not, you're a loser." The bleeding heart approach says "Don't worry dear, I'll help." Neither empowers the person to a sustained response.

Supportive challenge means being there for someone and staying there despite the setbacks; listening, encouraging, teaching, providing resources not available to the person at the time but also challenging the person to plan, figure out problems, understand and face consequences, and become active not passive. It also means helping that person to reenter the mainstream of life, become connected with other people and sources of support, and to learn survival skills and a process for responding to life. What it prevents is dependence on you, the helper, that eventually can become codependence, with you as the enabler. It is so easy to start out with good intentions to help, and gradually find yourself trapped in codependence. That, however, should never be used as an excuse to avoid helping when you know you can and should. Try supportive challenge instead.

*A*ctions

▲ There is a tendency to provide whatever the person needs either to keep him quiet, or out of a misguided brand of compassion. The other option is to say no and then get as far away as possible, so you don't get sucked in further. Is there someone in your life who frequently appears helpless? How do you respond?

▲ Supportive challenge is hard work, and it does not always succeed, but it is a hopeful place to start. Ask yourself what kinds of support the person needs that you can provide or, better still, help the person to achieve. How can you lovingly, strongly challenge someone to act positively, and do it over and over again? As you begin the supportive challenge journey, the most important clue is get as much help as possible for yourself. Spread out the responsibility so that you do not become overwhelmed.

*A*lbum

Déjà Vu; Crosby, Stills, Nash and Young; Atlantic SD 19118-2.

HOLD YOUR HEAD UP

▲ *(Argent/White)* ▲

Argent

Background

The roots of this song date back to the British invasion of 1964 when a group called the Zombies placed two terrific back-to-back hits on the U.S. charts. "She's Not There" and "Tell Her No" remain staples on oldies and classic-rock radio stations. Never quite equaling the impact of those early successes, the group broke up in 1969, but that isn't the end of the story. Famed performer and producer Al Kooper discovered a song of theirs called "Time of the Season." He urged his record company to release it as a single, and it became a huge hit even though the group had no plans or desire to get back together. Out of the ashes of the Zombies, a new group was born, called Argent, after Zombies' keyboardist/vocalist Rod Argent. Their third album *All Together Now* included the single "Hold Your Head Up," which went to number five on the charts in the summer of 1972.

Reflections

Do any of the following scenarios describe your life? From the time you can remember you felt put down by someone. Nothing was ever good enough. Perhaps you had a series of embarrassing failures in school. You were "one of them," a racial, ethnic, or religious minority growing up in a neighborhood of intolerance, or perhaps you grew up poor. In any of these situations and others too numerous to mention, you could not hold your head up. Every time you tried, you got a swat.

However, you survived, perhaps just barely, but you did, and that can give you something to build on. If you had any of those childhood experiences the first thing you need to do is congratulate yourself. You should not have had to live that way. No one should—but you did, and you made it. Feel proud.

The problem is that most of us who have these ensnaring roots hardly feel proud of our accomplishments. Instead, we feel angry, hurt, resentful, abandoned, and abused—and we are, or we were. Now, we no longer need to be any of that. With the right kind of support and challenge (see "Helpless" page 86) from others and, especially, from ourselves, we can break the hold that our past may have on us. We can see our tormentors, whoever they may have been, for what they really were: not all-powerful monsters, but weak, flawed people trapped in their own hell which they tried to pass on to us. It is a long road back to the self-esteem that allows us to hold our heads up, but, as in all other journeys, it begins with the first step.

You do not have to take the first step—you have already taken many steps. Recognize them! Rejoice in them! Then feel empowered to take the next step, whatever it is, and the next and the one after that.

*A*ctions

▲ Are you able to hold your head up most of the time, and feel proud of who you are and what you have done with your life? Yes? The appropriate response, then, is not any form of arrogance but rather a profound sense of thankfulness and a willingness to help others who still live with heads bent. If you've got it, give it away, and more will come to you.

▲ If you are still somewhere in the early part of the process of lifting your head up after a difficult childhood, an adult tragedy, or a series of major failures, don't be discouraged. First, get in touch with your strength, your successes, and whatever resilience has gotten you this far. Then, seek additional strength outside of yourself. Work with a friend or a counselor to develop a plan that will utilize your best qualities and help them to grow through a series of physical, mental, emotional, and spiritual exercises that will toughen your resilience and soften your shell of doubt and fear.

▲ Do you know anyone who might need a hand in strengthening their self-esteem? Can you do anything to reach out and lift their spirits?

*A*lbum

The Argent Anthology; Argent; Epic EK 33955.

HOMEWARD BOUND

▲ *(Simon)* ▲

Simon and Garfunkel

*B*ackground

In 1964, Simon and Garfunkel released their debut album *Wednesday Morning, 3 A.M.* It disappeared without a trace. Art Garfunkel enrolled in graduate school at Columbia University, and Paul Simon took off for England to perform as a solo artist. As the weeks turned into months, homesickness took its toll on Paul. Traveling from one gig to another, he found himself waiting for a train at a small railway station. To help pass the time, he began jotting down lyrics for a new song about his feelings; it was called "Homeward Bound." A year-and-a-half later, it became the followup single to "The Sounds of Silence," and climbed to number five on the charts.

*R*eflection

The longing for home that Paul Simon wrote and sang about so movingly is something to which we can all relate. In the early days of *Saturday Night Live*, one of the show's talented producers had an idea for the Christmas show. He set up a camera at a major metropolitan airport and shot reels of film of passengers arriving and meeting loved ones at the terminal. He caught image after image after image of weary, teary travelers returning home into the waiting arms of friends and family. They were all edited together to the voices of Simon and Garfunkel singing "Homeward Bound." The effect was very stirring and powerful.

Remember the blockbuster motion picture *E.T.?* It, too, was basically about that deep desire to return home. The lovable extraterrestrial left behind by its colleagues certainly appeared to enjoy all its adventures on a new planet but, in the end, the need to return home was overpowering. We've all had these feelings at different times in our lives. Whether it was at summer camp or going away to college or serving in the Armed Forces or leaving behind our families for an extended business trip, the desire to return home is often overwhelming. We'd like to suggest that somewhere deep in the core of each of us, there is a yearning to go home to a place that has nothing to do with geography as we know it. It is the desire to return home to the life force that put us here in the first place. It's our one true destination, that will answer once and for all the most baffling mysteries of the universe. In that sense, we are all on a journey, and we are all homeward bound.

*A*ctions

▲ When you are away from home for an extended period, on a vacation or a business trip, do you miss being home or do you dread coming home? If you dread it, what is so bad about your home? Is it the place itself (maybe you should move) or the people (that's more difficult, but maybe a move is appropriate) or is it you, your restlessness in being anyplace for very long, including in your own skin? (No, you can't move away from that, but you can learn to like yourself better).

▲ What are the qualities about your dwelling place that you most appreciate, that make it the home to which you want to return? What's missing? What can you do to make your place more of a home?

▲ Do you ever have a sense that your life is a journey to find your true home? Are there ever situations when you feel as though you have found that home, but then it slips away? That's all part of the journey. When you have these home-discovery experiences, savor them, remember them, be open to them.

*A*lbum

Collected Works; Simon and Garfunkel; Columbia C3K 45322.

HONESTY
▲ *(Joel)* ▲

Billy Joel

Background

Billy Joel hit his stride as a pop rock superstar with a string of mega success-ful albums in the midseventies. *The Stranger* in 1977, and *52nd Street* in 1978, established an enduring formula of lush ballads surrounded by out-and-out rockers that firmly entrenched Billy in the rock pantheon. Totally em-braced by album-rock radio, Billy nonetheless kept his fingers firmly on the pulse of top forty as well. Beginning with "Just the Way You Are" in 1977, Billy placed seven songs from those two albums on the American charts—four rockers and three ballads. "Honesty" was the third single release from *52nd Street* and climbed to number twenty-four in May 1979.

Reflection

What does it mean to be an honest person? It begins, of course, with a series of negatives: not lying, cheating, or stealing. What about the positive quali-ties of honesty? Are you honest not only on an ethical level of, say, financial dealing but also in the intricacies of personal relationships? Are you honest in revealing your feelings as well as your thoughts? Are you willing to be honest with someone even if it will harm your relationship?

Honesty is sometimes quite simple. It means admitting you did some-thing wrong, or giving back something that doesn't belong to you. It can also be tantalizingly complex when telling the truth or doing an honest deed can cause negative or unintended consequences.

Truth and honest deeds have a larger context that requires tact, care, and genuine love. Some true statements are really weapons used to hurt rather than heal; they would be better left unsaid or if said with love would have a very different meaning. Being an honest person means speaking the truth with love and respect, and attempting to be truthful not only about objective facts and opinions that are outside ourselves but also feelings, thoughts, and opinions that are within. That's something that none of us does fully. We can only continue to try.

*A*ctions

▲ What is the most dishonest thing you have ever done or statement you have ever made? Did you realize it at the time? When you did realize it, what did you do to correct it?

▲ Do you consider yourself usually an honest person in your dealings with others? If not, how can you change?

▲ Are you honest with yourself most of the time? Is there an area of your life in which you have not been so honest with yourself or anyone else: job, relationship, talents, and so forth? What can you do about it?

*A*lbum

52nd Street; Billy Joel; CBS CK 35609.

HOW CAN YOU MEND
A BROKEN HEART?
▲ *(B. Gibb/R. Gibb)* ▲

The Bee Gees

Background

The Bee Gees made their well-deserved entry into the Rock and Roll Hall of Fame in May 1997. With tongues planted firmly and characteristically in cheek, they described themselves as "the enigma with a stigma." This is because they became so identified with disco after the *Saturday Night Fever* phenomenon, that many rock 'n' roll purists dismissed them, while ignoring their earlier progressive-rock output. The brothers Gibb were caught, no pun intended, between a rock and a hard place. Disco brought them great wealth and fame even as it disintegrated their rock 'n' roll credibility. When the Hall of Fame beckoned, however, all was forgiven. The Bee Gees impressive string of nine number one singles began with "How Can You Mend a Broken Heart?" in August 1971.

Reflection

The first step in answering this question is to admit that your heart is broken. You can bury yourself in work as a distraction. You can hide behind a dozen different walls you cleverly create. You can feel solace or just the deadening of the pain through one or more addictive behaviors, but until you face your own brokenness no healing is likely to happen.

Share the pain with at least one person who is a good, sensitive listener. Let that person know that you are not seeking answers but only a sympathetic ear. That takes the burden off the person to problem solve—a tendency most of us have that may not be what you need. In the course of the conversation, important clues will emerge, but usually from you rather than the listener. The very telling of the story to someone who really listens is often the best step to healing. When you reflect on the conversation later, insights about your feelings may emerge.

Allow yourself to feel the pain. Get it out! Shout it out! Seek comfort in the experiences that you find lifegiving: walks on the beach or in the woods, music, sports, prayer and meditation, humor, and physical and intellectual creativity. When your heart breaks, a part of you dies. You need to mourn that loss appropriately without wallowing in self-pity and, gradually, allow yourself to come back to a full life. Do not ever underestimate the destructive power of a broken heart or the heart's capacity to recreate itself, stronger than ever.

Actions

▲ Is your heart broken? Have you admitted the extent of the brokenness to yourself or are you denying it?

▲ How are you dealing with your broken heart? Have you found ways to "get it out—let it out" that are helpful? Are there people who are good listeners for you? Do you seek them out?

▲ Are you blaming yourself in some way for your broken heart? Do you need to forgive yourself? Do you believe that you even deserve forgiveness? You do! Believe it!

▲ Do you know someone whose heart has been broken? Are you willing to be there, to listen with your heart?

Album

Best of the Bee Gees, Volume 2; The Bee Gees; Polydor 831 960-2.

HUNGRY HEART
▲ *(Springsteen)* ▲

Bruce Springsteen

*B*ackground

By the late seventies, Bruce Springsteen appeared to have the rock world by the tail. He had already been proclaimed rock 'n' roll's future, and his albums were immediate and longlasting successes, played endlessly on FM rock stations across the country. One traditional measure of success eluded him—the top-forty singles chart. "Born to Run" barely cracked the top thirty, making it to number twenty-three in 1975. "Prove It All Night" from *Darkness on the Edge of Town* went to number thirty-three in 1978. That was it. Until 1980, that is. Springsteen peppered his two-record set *The River* with memorable potential singles, as well as lengthy album tracks. His record company put a lot of muscle behind the album's first single release, and Bruce finally had his first of many top ten recordings. It was "Hungry Heart," which climbed to number five in early 1981.

*R*eflection

Hunger for food can drive a person to rob or kill. It can also drive someone completely crazy. Beyond violence or madness is a totally debilitating motionlessness that is the inevitable prelude to a painful death, unless someone intervenes.

The hunger of the heart can be just as disturbing and all consuming. What of the heart that seems to be in its death throes, bereft of all movement except the incessant thumping of its simultaneous hardening and emptying? Just as the emaciated body of a person deprived of food can be brought back to life through proper nourishment, so, too, can a hungry heart that has been endlessly starved for affection be revived by love.

Each of us, in some way, at some time, has a hungry heart. The hunger or longing may be in the midst of plenty and can cause even a well-adjusted person to lose all for a desire that has become an obsession. Usually though, the hunger is caused by a lack of nurturing, the slow deterioration of a previously vibrant relationship, a sudden betrayal or loss of legitimate power, or the gradual ebbing of self-confidence that may result from a series of emotional walls or barriers, and then produce more of the same. The result in each situation is a heart that is still hungry, but is, for a time, without the capacity to seek nourishment. That can happen to any one of us. The danger comes when emptiness becomes a habit of the heart, when the heart ceases to feel and becomes a hard, empty shell. Until that moment though, hope remains for the hungry heart.

*A*ctions

▲ What are the hungers of your heart: your family, your lover, your friends, using your creativity, your profession, helping others, seeking justice, or, perhaps, becoming whole again after your heart has been broken? These are all positive kinds of hunger. The problem arises when they begin to compete for heart food like a nest of hungry chicks snapping at whatever the hen has to offer. Where are you feeling the pressure now in your life? Have you given in to the hungriest demand from say your job or the neediest person in your life? How can you restore the balance?

▲ Suppose your heart is in just the opposite situation—empty, isolated. How can you become reconnected to meaning and to personal relationships? Try to build on what is already there. You may say there is nothing, but you are wrong. There are interests and talents in you, however neglected or suppressed. There are relationships, however negative or sterile. Start there and, if all else fails, start somewhere completely different.

*A*lbum

The River; Bruce Springsteen; Columbia CK2 36854.

I BELIEVE IN YOU

▲ *(Young)* ▲

Neil Young

Background

Neil Young has enjoyed one of the most spectacular careers in all rock 'n' roll history. Beginning with the Buffalo Springfield in the sixties, he has left his mark on each succeeding decade and each succeeding generation of rock musicians and rock audiences. Neil Young has attempted nearly every genre of rock 'n' roll music and mastered just about every one of them. Diversity is his calling card. His breakthrough solo album was the 1970 classic *After the Gold Rush*. It displayed the complete range of his enormous talents from raging rocker, as evidenced by songs such as "Southern Man," to sensitive singer-songwriter exemplified by the beautiful "I Believe in You."

Reflection

If you have ever had anyone say this to you, be it a parent, teacher, counselor, coach, spiritual advisor, employer, friend, or lover, you have indeed received a great gift. These very words can change your life. They have that kind of power.

How many stories have you heard about a special person in the life of a child whose belief in the talents or intelligence or goodness of that child have turned his/her life around? How many times have you heard someone say that falling in love radically changed that person's life? For the very first time, someone said, "I believe in you." Life is changed forever.

The real question is, of course, do you believe in you? When someone else tells you, "I believe in you," they offer you a great gift that can make the difference between a life of self-esteem, achievement, and even happiness, and a life of self-doubt, repeated failures, and depression. The catch is, you have to accept the gift and allow its power to enter your life and fill you with a positive sense of yourself. Otherwise, the words will ring hollow for you.

Why are some people so resistant to praise, love, and acceptance? Usually there is a history of abuse, abandonment, betrayal, or repeated tragedy. Sometimes it almost seems genetic, as though some mysterious chromosome has entered the body that resists the exorcism of love and praise. One thing is certain. Repetition does aid comprehension, not only in teaching, but also in helping someone believe in his or herself. Hearing "I believe in you" over and over again accompanied by positive supportive deeds may someday produce "I believe in myself."

*A*ctions

▲ Is there anyone who has said "I believe in you" to you in a way that strongly influenced your life? Try to recall the importance of those words and how they motivated you.

▲ Is there anyone who says that to you now? Can you accept the gift? What effect does it have on you?

▲ Do you say the words "I believe in you" to anyone in your life? Do you feel as though your words are accepted? When they do not seem to be, what do you do? Do you stop or continue, undeterred by the apparent rejection?

▲ Think of one person in your life who needs to know that you believe in them. Try saying it and showing it.

*A*lbum

After the Gold Rush; Neil Young; Reprise 2283-2.

I CAN SEE CLEARLY NOW

▲ *(Nash)* ▲

Johnny Nash

*B*ackground

You've been around for a while if you remember that Johnny Nash was a member of Arthur Godfrey's television family for seven years. At various times in a long career, Johnny dabbled with gospel, pop, soul, show tunes, and easy-listening music before scoring big with the new sound bubbling up from Jamaica in the late sixties and early seventies. It was called *reggae,* and one of its foremost practitioners was Bob Marley. Nash scored a couple of successes with songs written by Marley but, then, in 1972, he went to Jamaica to write and record with Marley's backup group the Wailers. One song from those sessions contained an irresistibly positive message and an equally infectious rhythm. "I Can See Clearly Now" soared to the top of the charts in November 1972.

*R*eflection

You're walking along the street and *wham!* suddenly you get it. You wake up one morning and the jumbled mass of conflicts from the previous day are untangled, at least in your mind. You have been working on a problem or a project for months and, little by little, the pieces of the puzzle fit into place. You finally understand the whole thing. You can see clearly now.

What a great feeling, that moment of insight, but how do those aha! moments happen? No one knows exactly, but there are some clues. The first one is hard work, plugging away at something until you get it. The second seems like a direct contradiction. It calls for stopping the pursuit for a while and concentrating somewhere else, maybe taking a few hours or days or weeks off from the task at hand and doing something completely different, something recreative. You can get all tied up in knots when you are trying to figure something out. Taking a swim, a walk in the woods, playing or listening to music, a long talk with a close friend, or just being quiet for a while can relax whatever it was in your brain or in your heart that was blocking you from seeing clearly. Try it!

There is one caution in this process. The first burst of insight is not necessarily the last: Just when you thought you had the whole thing figured out, something else will pop up that is complementing or perhaps contradicting the original message. Stay tuned. Let the creative juices flow. It sounds like you're on a roll. Don't forget that original powerful blast from your subconscious. Keep reflecting on it, and see if what was clear is now even clearer.

$\mathcal{A}$ctions

▲ Do some time-traveling in your mind and remember past experiences you have had of being stumped about a problem in your work or in a relationship. How did the breakthrough happen? Try to get a feel for it by getting in touch with the process of the breakthrough, and also the feelings you had then.

▲ Life at times seems to be a series of unclear choices and barely inaccessible solutions to complex problems. You're almost there, but not quite. You see it, but then it fades away before you can really grasp it. Don't be surprised. Life is like that, but don't give up. Stay in the flow, stay focused on the problem or the vision you are trying to see. When it seems hopeless or you are exhausted, take a break. Go somewhere else in your mind or with your feet. When you come back you may be pleasantly surprised.

$\mathcal{A}$lbum

Billboard Top Rock 'n' Roll Hits—1972; Various Artists; Rhino R2 70633.

I CAN'T STOP LOVING YOU

▲ *(Gibson)* ▲

Ray Charles

*B*ackground

Ray Charles was already a big star with two number-one singles to his credit when he began seeking a new direction for his music in 1962. He asked his producer to gather together a collection of the best country songs of the last twenty years. Impressed by what he heard, Ray went into the studio, and against the advice of his record company, recorded *Modern Sounds in Country and Western Music.* It became one of his biggest albums ever, and the first gold album in the history of ABC-Paramount Records. A Don Gibson song from 1958, "I Can't Stop Loving You" became Ray's third number-one single in June of 1962.

*R*eflection

Statistics would seem to indicate that most marriages end in divorce. The truth is that seventy percent of first marriages survive. It's when you add in the people who have two or more marriages that the number goes under half. What a joy it is when you have been married for thirty or forty or fifty years, are still in love, and love each other more now because of all the years shared. Yes, these marriages do exist.

The long-term loving couples whom we encounter are usually far from perfect, but they have somehow managed to find the secret of staying together. It starts with a genuine admiration for one other, and a recognition of being loved despite faults, limitations, and insecurities. What a great feeling it is to have a partner who truly knows you and loves you despite whatever insufficiencies you have, a partner who does not focus on your weaknesses and try to pick them and you apart piece by piece, but rather supports you, listens to you, and is there for you. It is possible to have that kind of relationship. You need to be clear about it with your partner from the beginning, and come back to it again and again. By the way, it is also an incredible sexual turn on, the ultimate in safe sex, and a journey into true ecstasy, all at the same time.

ctions

▲ When love is fresh and new, it seems as though it will go on that way forever; it is that strong and intense. Don't be fooled! It can develop into a positive "I Can't Stop Loving You" relationship if both of you are open to give and receive deeply, if you work hard to always stay in touch with each other emotionally, and if you are willing to forgive each other and yourselves. Plan at least one step you can take in that direction in your most important relationship.

▲ If you sense there is something going wrong in your relationship, even though the relationship is still basically strong, try to deal with it without blowing it out of proportion. Always come back to affirm the positives you share. If you don't, you may find them slipping away.

lbum

Modern Sounds in Country and Western Music; Ray Charles; Rhino 70099.

I FEEL FREE

▲ *(Bruce/Brown)* ▲

Cream

Background

They took the music world by storm in 1967. Ginger Baker, Jack Bruce, and Eric Clapton—Cream! Just three guys whose combined sound was bigger, badder, harder, louder, and larger than groups twice their size. Baker's drumming, Bruce's bass, and Clapton's extraordinary guitar playing captured the ears of the world in a year that also saw the rise of the Jimi Hendrix Experience and the Doors, the release of *Sgt. Pepper's Lonely Hearts Club Band,* the Monterey International Pop Festival, and the summer of love. Against this backdrop, the music of Cream was infectious and exhilarating. Side one, cut one, of their first American release, *Fresh Cream,* provided young people with an anthem that captured the spirit of what was happening all around the globe. It was called "I Feel Free."

Reflection

What does it mean to feel free? For tens of millions of immigrants fleeing political, social, religious, or economic oppression, it has meant coming to the United States to start a new life. On a personal level, real freedom can begin with overcoming an addiction, leaving an abusive relationship, or finding a new job that frees your creativity. The danger in these supposedly liberating moves is that you can jump from the frying pan into the fire, tossing off one form of oppression for a more insidious version. What looked like salvation becomes a new model of entrapment.

Personal freedom begins with a series of freedoms *from:* persecution, abuse, addictions, poverty, etc. It must also include freedoms *for:* creativity, relationships, healing and nurturing. These freedoms arise from within, but only after certain constraints are removed or overcome. Then, a new sense of freedom emerges. A burden has been taken off your shoulders. You feel like you finally have your life together and it is your life, not somebody else's version of your life with the other person in control. No! You are in control and you experience a wholeness to your life that was never there before, a peaceful confidence and excitement all at the same time. Sure, it could all be shattered into a hundred pieces tomorrow, but don't keep looking back over your shoulder, look ahead and enjoy your feeling of freedom. If you use it well it will only grow stronger.

Actions

▲ For most of us there are whole areas of our life in which we are not free. Even when we do feel free, the shadows of oppression still loom. In what places in your life do you feel a lack of legitimate freedom? Do you know the causes of this condition? If so, what are you doing to get out from under these constraints? What do you need to do now?

▲ There are other parts of you or other situations in your life in which you do feel free. How did you achieve these freedoms? Go back and trace the path of freedom in your life, how you struggled on your own to get there and how others helped you. What can you learn from these freedom journeys that you might apply to areas of your life that are still all locked up or locked out?

Album

The Very Best of Cream; Cream; Polydor 31452 2752-2.

I HEARD IT THROUGH THE GRAPEVINE

(Whitfield/Strong)

▲ *Marvin Gaye*

Background

"I Heard It Through the Grapevine" is one of Motown's most enduring success stories. It had already been recorded by the Miracles and the Isley Brothers when Gladys Knight and the Pips took it to number two on the charts in December 1967. Exactly one year later, Marvin Gaye's reworking of the song went straight to number one and stayed there for seven weeks—one of the longest reigns at the top of the charts for any Motown recording. Creedence Clearwater Revival recorded an eleven-minute version of the song in 1970 for *Cosmo's Factory.* An edited single made the charts in 1976, long after the group had disbanded. Other artists who have recorded it include the Temptations, Ike and Tina Turner, and Elton John. Pssst . . . it's a great song. . . . pass it on!

Reflection

Were you really the last to know? Everyone else seemed to know; they saw the signs that you were too blind or trusting or just too busy to see. Now that you heard it through the proverbial grapevine you finally do know the sad truth. You've been had!

This song is obviously about a betrayal in love but there are other situations to which it could also be applied. You just got fired and you never saw it coming. Your business partner has been robbing you blind. Your best friend has spread your secret told in strict confidence all over town. The grade, position, or prize that you have been trying hard to achieve was never really within grasp. Everyone always knew it, except you.

How can you avoid being blindsided, see it coming, and prevent the worst damage? Let's face it, sometimes you can't. Sometimes you can only do damage control after the grapevine has wrapped itself around you and broken your heart. There are some warning signs that can tip you off if you are tuned in. The problem is, they are often hard to read, veiled in deceptive verbiage or avoidance. The best advice in these matters is to be trustworthy yourself, in love and in life, and let it be known that you expect nothing less in return. It is amazing how trust builds upon trust, so that even when betrayal happens in one relationship, there are other trusting relationships to cushion the fall.

Suppose you are on the other end of the grapevine. If you are falling out of love with someone, have the guts to say it, with as much kindness and tact as possible. Don't wait until the revelation comes through a third party. As painful as it may be for both of you, have the courage to say it face-to-face.

$\mathcal{A}$ctions

▲ Have you or are you about to hurt someone, or perhaps end the relationship? How can you do it with the least harm?

▲ If you are hearing rumors through the grapevine that you're being cheated upon in some way, what should you do? How can you check it out? If you determine that there is some truth to the rumors, what is the next move?

▲ Suppose you hear something about someone else that's not true. Will you intervene to protect that person's reputation, or just let it pass?

$\mathcal{A}$lbum

Anthology; Marvin Gaye; Motown MCD06199MD2.

IMAGINE
▲ (Lennon) ▲
John Lennon

Background

There are only four people in the history of the world who truly know what it was like to be a Beatle. When the group self-destructed in early 1970, those four individuals had to reinvent themselves as well as reorient their careers. In some respects, John Lennon had the most difficult time of it. Because of his legendary past, just about anything he put out became a hit, but he didn't find his true voice as a solo artist until the release of the single and album entitled *Imagine* in 1971. The song articulated a vision that John and his wife Yoko Ono had been attempting to live out in their personal and professional lives. The song instantly connected with a mass audience and rose to number three on the charts. If possible, it has become even more meaningful and poignant since John's passing in 1980.

Reflection

Albert Einstein said that imagination is more powerful than knowledge. It is true that knowledge is power, but imagination gives us the greatest power of all: the power to create. Imagination allows us suddenly to see old truths in a new light. Connections that never occurred to us before suddenly appear before our eyes. Problems that were unsolvable quickly fall into place when the power of imagination works its magic. Most important, imagination allows us to enter the mystery, to journey beyond what appears to be to what truly is and what could be. If we exercise the powers of our imagination we can never be fully enslaved by anything or anyone. There will always be that part of us that remains uncontrolled.

Imagination can provide us with sudden powerful bursts of energy or creativity that send us charging into the battles of life, or it can nurture us gradually, building our inner strength so that we may finally act decisively.

Imagination is also our constant companion through boredom, depression, confusion, stress, and even betrayal. The question is, how do we use this remarkable gift for our best advantage and greatest benefit to others?

Actions

▲ Some people use their imagination to create their own interior world that cuts them off from the outer world, and acts like a kind of permanent cocoon. Most of us use our imagination to bring out the best in ourselves to share with the outside world.

▲ Think of some positive ways that you have used your imagination to create, to solve problems, or to help someone. Spend some time remembering those experiences and delighting in them.

▲ How do you use your imagination every day? Does your job call for imagination? How can you use it to make your work more interesting and rewarding? What are the other ways you use your imagination: at home, in your relationships, in hobbies, or just for you?

▲ Allow yourself to imagine. Most of your imaginings will remain just that, but some of them will lead to other adventures. Even more important, the act of imagining can be an end in itself, a glorious journey into a world that can be.

Album

The John Lennon Collection; John Lennon; Capitol CDP 7 9156 2.

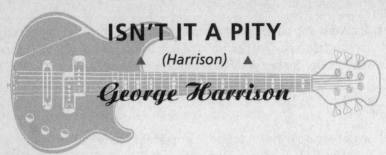

ISN'T IT A PITY

▲ *(Harrison)* ▲

George Harrison

*B*ackground

In the very earliest days of the Beatles, each member of the group got stamped with a very specific image. John was "the leader," Paul was "the cute one," George was "the serious one," and Ringo was "the funny one." *A Hard Day's Night* solidified these identities in the public consciousness and, now, over thirty years later, they still accurately capture thumbnail sketches of the Beatles' personalities. Paul is still the cute one, Ringo is still the funny one, and George is definitely the serious one. That seriousness carried over into Harrison's solo career right from the very first album: *All Things Must Pass* contained songs about God, love, life, death, and human frailty. One of the most poignant was "Isn't It a Pity."

*R*eflection

George Harrison is right. It is a pity. It is a shame. We do break both hearts and vows. We do cause pain. We do go on our merry way and forget to give back, forget to be thankful for all we have been given. Harrison's newfound spirituality made him acutely aware of this tragic dimension of the human condition, and this song is a fervent plea for a more mindful and soulful human response. His concern is not only on the level of individual behavior but also expanding to families and communities and countries.

As we have seen the wholesale slaughter of millions in Cambodia and Rwanda, and the slightly smaller genocides of Timor and Bosnia during the past quarter century, his words seem to have fallen on deaf ears. Even in our own supposedly safe and free environment, we have record statistics of family violence and random killings.

There is no simple solution but there is a starting point. People must be held accountable! Each of us is accountable for our own actions and the consequences of those actions. We may not have the power to bring political op-pressors or genocidal killers to trial, or to bring the driveby murderers of chil-dren to justice. We must, however, not be silent and passive: that gives them both immunity and a newfound power to kill. We need to raise our voices and connect them to the all-too-silent chorus through groups in our commu-nity, in the halls of the United Nations, and in Washington. Finally, we can take personal responsibility for all the pain we have caused and hearts we have broken. Instead of wallowing in guilt, we can offer repentance in what-ever form is appropriate and seek forgiveness in whatever manner is possible.

*A*ctions

▲ Is there some grave injustice on a national or international level that has really angered you? If not, wake up! A part of your humanity has become anesthetized by the serial violence you have seen on TV or read about in the paper. If you have felt the horror and frustration, it's time to do some-thing about it. Connect your caring spirit to a human-rights group that is actually making a difference.

▲ Is there someone in your life that you have hurt severely? What can you do to make amends? How can you change your behavior so that it does not happen again?

▲ Do you know someone who has been badly abused, either physically or emotionally or who has experienced some kind of injustice? Do you feel compassion for that person? What have you done about it? If you feel awkward or embarrassed, get over it and, for openers, just try to be there for that person.

*A*lbum

All Things Must Pass; George Harrison; Capitol CDP 7 46688 2.

ISN'T SHE LOVELY
▲ (Wonder) ▲
Stevie Wonder

Background

Many of us have had the great privilege of watching Stevie Wonder grow from a thirteen-year-old musical prodigy into a fully matured adult superstar. Throughout his teen years, he unleashed a torrent of soulful pop confections that consistently landed him in the upper reaches of the charts. He was the pride of Motown, who literally grew up before our eyes and ears. As he entered his twenties, his music began to subtly shift and change. Beginning with *Music of My Mind* in 1972, his albums displayed a maturity beyond his years and a seriousness not even hinted at in his earlier work. He was overflowing with ideas and music that poured out in an incredible trilogy of LPs: *Talking Book, Innervisions,* and *Songs in the Key of Life,* each one surpassing and outdistancing the last. He was writing about his life, and one of the things that happened to him was fatherhood. He couldn't contain his pride and joy, and it all came spilling out into a wonderful song called "Isn't She Lovely."

Reflection

Remember that magical moment when you first saw your child, your niece or nephew, or your best friend's baby? Words like lovely, gorgeous, beautiful, and magnificent were in the air, coming from the heart. There is something truly wonder-filled about a new baby, a generous burst of life suddenly appearing in our universe. It is enough to gladden the hearts of all but the most perverse.

You probably still remember the wonder, the "isn't she lovely" moment of ecstasy, all those tender moments of closeness with children in your life, the joy of discovery, the exuberance of energy, the warmth of the deep, powerful hugs, the smiles that light up the room and light up your heart. You know that the spirit of children is what helps keep you alive and prevents you from becoming old before your time. Yes, they can be demanding. Yes, you have to make constant sacrifices. The rewards far surpass all that, but only if you do not seek them, only if you keep your heart open to these treasures of the universe, even as they may be breaking your heart.

*A*ctions

▲ If you have children, take a moment each day to gaze on them and find simple ways to connect with their inner beauty through a smile, a warm greeting, a hug, an attentive conversation, or a special kindness. It may be hard to be aware enough to do it at first, but if you stay with it you will get in the groove.

▲ If you are alienated from them, remember happier times and discover a way back into the relationship. Be willing to put aside your pride to take the first step, even though you may have a fear of rejection.

▲ If you have no children of your own, do something about it by deepening your relationship with nieces, nephews, neighbors, cousins, or the children of your friends. Consider going one step further and becoming a mentor or a Big Brother or Sister to a child that needs a significant adult relationship.

▲ Rediscover the child inside you. Allow your playfulness to reemerge. Spend time with friends who have that forever young quality. Maybe some of it will rub off (See "Forever Young," p. 66).

*A*lbum

Songs in the Key of Life; Stevie Wonder; Motown 3746303403.

IT DON'T COME EASY
▲ *(Starkey)* ▲

Ringo Starr

Background

Who could have guessed it? For years he was the butt of Beatles' jokes concerning his relative importance to the group measured against his more prolific bandmates. However, Ringo Starr emerged after the breakup as one of the most successful ex-Beatles, placing hit after hit after hit on the U.S. charts. Many of these were remakes of old rock 'n' roll hits such as "You're Sixteen." Others were songs written for Ringo by such old friends as Harry Nilsson and George Harrison; some of them were written by Ringo himself exhibiting all the wit, charm, and cleverness that we had come to expect from "the funny Beatle" over the years. He had obviously learned a thing or two in the company of his celebrated bandmates. "It Don't Come Easy" peaked at number four on the U.S. charts in June 1971.

Reflection

You may think it should come easy. It seems to come easy for other people, why not for me? Why is it always so hard for me?

The "it" in this title can apply to anything or to life itself. There are some people for whom life does seem to be easy. They get it. They don't seem to struggle. They bounce back from adversity. What is their secret?

Most of the seemingly easy-come people have high self-esteem. They are not always worried about the next disaster just over the horizon. They believe that they are lovable and are loved. They have a zest for life, and are actively engaged in it rather than being spectators. Having said all that, though, usually they are also hard workers, not afraid to take chances, and have a clear focus and determination to succeed. Even for them, success does not really come easy.

There is a presumption in our society that things should come easy. They do for the superstars, the apparent role models of society who glitter and glisten on society pages, in commercials, and at gala events. They are paid well for their one-dimensional talent. It all looks so easy.

There is a satisfaction though, in giving it your all, focusing your attention, dealing with a series of adversities and seeing something through to completion. In the end, someone may say that it came easy for you, but you know that "it don't come easy," it only seems that way. You also know that if you were only willing to attempt what is easy, life would be boring, and so would you.

Actions

▲ If you feel that nothing comes easy for you, ask yourself why. Is it an attitude of fear or insecurity in you that sets you up for failure or at least unnecessary setbacks? Try to target the cause of the difficulty and begin to take some small steps to counter it.

▲ Remember an experience in which you succeeded against great odds, with a great deal of hard work and dedication. The next time you're in a tough spot, remember that you once came through with flying colors and that you can do it again.

Album

Blast From Your Past; Ringo Starr; Parlophone CDP 7 46663 2.

IT'S ONLY ROCK 'N' ROLL

▲ *(Jagger/Richards)* ▲

The Rolling Stones

Background

Rock 'n' roll has always been very self-referential music. Rock 'n' roll songs about rock 'n' roll are legion. Even the first number one hit of the rock era—"Rock Around the Clock" by Bill Haley and the Comets—is about the music itself. Almost every major star or group has attempted one: Chuck Berry in the fifties, the Animals in the sixties, Bob Seger in the seventies, and John Mellancamp in the eighties, have all written great anthems about rock 'n' roll. So it comes as no surprise that the greatest rock 'n' roll band in the world would take a stab at one—and be very successful at it. "It's Only Rock 'n' Roll" by the Rolling Stones went to number sixteen on the U.S. charts in the summer of 1974.

Reflection

Fifty-thousand people of all ages, sizes, shapes, and colors pay between sixty and four-hundred dollars a ticket to sit in Giant Stadium on a cold October night to watch a bunch of fifty-plus dissipated-looking rockers drive them wild. From the first two beats of the first number they get much more than "Satisfaction." By the second song they are caught up in the magical frenzy that we know to be rock 'n' roll. Do they like it? You bet!

What is it that has been captivating teenagers for more than forty years, and now provides the same mesmerizing mania to near-senior citizens? What is at the root cause of its powerful, transforming presence?

The best of rock 'n' roll, as served up by Mick Jagger and the Rolling Stones, assaults the body, mind, and soul with a surging life force that grabs you by the gut and won't let go. It calls you into another world that is less in-hibited and wilder than your everyday life. It enlivens your sources of energy, and shakes you loose from your insecurities, problems, and boredom, if only for a few hours or even a few minutes when you hear a favorite song on the radio. It may arouse sexual passion that was slumbering, and it may even bring the touch of that all too infrequent guest, pure joy.

Rock 'n' roll is a turn on in so many different ways, an invitation to new dimensions of freedom. But in the end, it is only rock 'n' roll. It is not salvation as many have believed, especially as did its first generation of true believers, but it is a force that helped to change that generation and beyond. It is also a vehicle for many of the greatest poets of our century and a legion of uncommon-sense philosophers, psychologists, and, occasionally, theologians. Their wisdom, however, is almost always second fiddle or, more appropriately, backup guitar, to the sheer weight of the music itself and its infectious beat.

All legitimate art brings us true wisdom about life itself and our role in it. For all of its raucous and rowdy pounding of our senses, rock 'n' roll is its own genuine art form and carries its own wisdom. Lest it be lost in the endless repetition of a relatively few oldies hits and the crass commercialism of the big business it has become, let us pause for a few minutes to listen anew to one-hundred pieces of rock wisdom. We will share our reflections on them, but because each is a work of art in its own way, you may hear your own very different impressions and insights. At the very least, we hope you will be touched by their wisdom and make it part of your own. Contrary to what your elders have told you, the term rock wisdom is not an oxymoron. Long may it live on!

*A*ctions

 Send us your list of rock wisdom song titles that we may have missed or not had room for at this time. You never know, there may be a next time. Send all suggestions to:

> Bill Ayres and Pete Fornatale
> c/o World Hunger Year
> 505 8th Avenue, 21st Floor
> New York, NY 10018

*A*lbum

It's Only Rock 'n' Roll; The Rolling Stones; Virgin 39523.

JUST THE WAY YOU ARE

▲ *(Joel)* ▲

Billy Joel

Background

One can easily imagine the mixed blessing this song has been in the career of Billy Joel. On the one hand, it was a huge hit, rocketing into the top ten from *The Stranger* album in the winter of 1978. On the other hand, it's a pretty schmaltzy signature song for one who envisions himself as such a dyed-in-the-wool rock 'n' roller. Billy's self-image notwithstanding, it is a beautiful song that struck a responsive chord in the hearts of lovers the world over. Unfortunately, life doesn't always follow the script we write for ourselves. In Billy's case, he is long since divorced from the woman for whom he originally wrote the song, but countless other couples have adopted it as their own and strive daily to live up to its mighty high ideals. Also, its appeal is multi-generational. For the best example of this, check out Frank Sinatra's version on the *Trilogy* album, recorded in 1980.

Reflection

Saying that you love someone "just the way you are," and meaning it, is one of the most difficult statements anyone can make. After all, everyone has faults, those annoying little habits or eccentricities that can drive you crazy, or worse, fears, insecurities, or ego that produce behavior that is unpleasant or even harmful. If you were being honest wouldn't you have to say that there are things you would like to change about your partner? So, how can you say what Billy Joel says in this song without being a hypocrite?

The answer to that most challenging question revolves around accepting the core of someone's being, discovering the beauty and goodness of a person and being so attracted to that vibrant, radiant center that all else becomes meaningless. The other part of the equation is that, at the same time, you feel loved and accepted in a way that you never have felt before. The feeling is intoxicating, transforming, and, yes, blinding. You can become blind to faults that are obvious to others. You are drawn like a magnet to the center of that special person and, in turn, they are drawn to you. Your centers hold. All else is detail. You can say, "I love you just the way you are" and mean it with all your heart.

What happens as time goes on is that the magnetic force loses some of its power. The centers fade and do not hold. The warts of personality appear, and begin to take center stage. "If only she would change the way she talks," "If only he would change the way he acts," can eventually become, "Change the way you are. You are not good enough." Before things unravel that far, go back to your center, the center of your goodness, who you really are. Then look again at your beloved and remember who it was that you loved, "just the way you are."

Actions

▲ If you are fortunate enough to have a just-the-way-you-are relationship, do not assume it will stay that way without some work.

▲ What acts of generosity, caring, passion, or forgiveness can you perform on a regular basis to help maintain the connection between your center and that of your lover?

▲ Are you staying in touch with each other on a deep enough level, or are you backing away into your own worlds? Do you still have common interests and concerns? Do you spend time with each other and really listen to each other?

▲ If something is bothering you about your partner do you say so in a way that can be heard and appreciated, not dismissed as part of an ongoing stream of criticism and complaints? Can your partner do the same for you? If not, try to set aside some uninterrupted time for conversation focused on the problem.

Album

The Stranger; Billy Joel; CBS CK 34987.

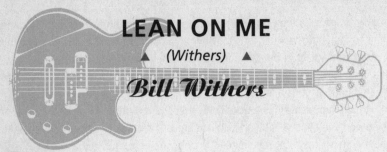

LEAN ON ME

▲ *(Withers)* ▲

Bill Withers

*B*ackground

It seems that one sure path to the top of the music charts in America is to write a song about being there for somebody. "Bridge Over Troubled Water," "You've Got A Friend," "Stand By Me," and "Reach Out I'll Be There" all made it to number one. So did "Lean on Me" by Bill Withers in July of 1972. Withers is another unlikely pop star on our list. His last job before embarking on a successful music career was making toilet seats for 747 airplanes! In his spare time, he worked on his songwriting and guitar playing. He was introduced to Booker T. Washington of Booker T. and the MGs, who agreed to produce his debut album *Just As I Am* for Sussex Records. It contained two solid hit singles, "Ain't No Sunshine" and "Grandma's Hands"and paved the way for Wither's second album *Still Bill,* which included "Lean on Me."

*R*eflection

This is one of the most loving, heartfelt, and healing songs in contemporary music. Every time you hear it you can feel embraced, comforted, supported, and affirmed, all at the same time. Play it when you are feeling down and allow its compassion to fill you and touch you on the deep levels where you hurt.

If you say the words "lean on me" to someone, you had better mean them, and be willing to accept the consequences. The goal of the offer should always be empowerment and renewal, supporting someone emotionally, physically, spiritually, or financially for a period of time. The danger is that you can become an enabler and promote dependence rather than independence (see page 86 for our discussion of supportive challenge in "Helpless").

If what develops is legitimate support that is helping a person become strong and whole again, know that you are doing a wonderful thing. The burden will be there, but it will be more than compensated if you can be in touch with the power of the healing that you are promoting. Rejoice in it! Be thankful that you can give it. Most important, remember the time will come when you will need someone to lean on. Hopefully, that person will be there for you and you will not be too proud to accept the help. Thus, the cycle will continue of mutual support because the wisdom of the song is real. We do all need someone to lean on and we never, never know when the need will appear again.

*A*ctions

▲ Are you usually willing to go out of your way for a friend, family member, or colleague to lean on you for a while? Is it usually a good experience for you? What problems have you had in helping this way? What rewards? What have you learned from these experiences?

▲ If you have had some bad experiences of people taking advantage of you, learn from the experience but try not to let it discourage you from being willing to help someone else.

▲ If there is someone who needs you to lean on for a while, try to be available without promoting codependency.

*A*lbum

Bill Withers' Greatest Hits; Bill Withers; Columbia CK 37199.

LET IT BE
▲ *(Lennon/McCartney)* ▲

The Beatles

Background

Once the Beatles were launched in their own private spaceship to stardom, nearly everything they did was recorded, photographed, and documented. This extended to their inevitable disintegration in 1970. The threads had already begun to unravel when the group decided to fulfill a movie contract by allowing a film crew to observe the band at work in the studio on a new album. The camera caught more than it bargained for. It captured the breaking up of the Beatles. Yet, even under these most trying of circumstances, they managed to make magical and meaningful music. The film, the soundtrack album, and one of its biggest hit singles were all titled "Let It Be."

Reflection

In an age of quick-fix painkillers and clear-cut solutions to extraordinarily complex problems presented on TV in less than an hour, let it be is suspect wisdom—at best. More often than not, action seems to be the right choice. Act now! Do something, anything, before the situation gets worse. Get involved! Don't be a passive spectator.

Yet, we all know there are situations that call for a calm, reflective approach. You let it be for a while, as you try to figure out the problem and gather all the resources you need from within you and around you to be effective. If you move precipitously you will fail.

What about a situation that goes beyond a mere problem and enters into the world of mystery, the world beyond your control but not beyond your influence? It may have to do with a relationship that is falling apart or someone's life that is falling apart, including your own. You have done all you can do and, still, you know there is more. There must be more! How do you overcome this terrible feeling of powerlessness?

*A*ctions

▲ Let it be for a while. Stop trying to figure it out on the level of problem-solving, and allow yourself to enter a place of trust where answers will come, if you listen. They may not be the answers you expect or the ones you have put time and energy and money into, but they will be given to you.

▲ Instead of obsessively worrying about a problem, focus your attention elsewhere. Take a walk, listen to music, go to a movie, read a book, exercise vigorously, anything to get you into a different space. Sometimes, when you come back to the problem, you have a fresh perspective that allows you to see options that did not appear before.

▲ At other times, the walls are still there, and you still feel trapped and powerless. It may be that in this area of your life you are powerless in the traditional sense of the term, but remember, there is strength in weakness. It's not usually a pleasant experience but it can be a transforming one. It can change your life, if you can just let it be.

*A*lbum

Let It Be; the Beatles; Parlophone CDP 7 46447 2.

LET IT GROW
▲ *(Clapton)* ▲

Eric Clapton

Background

Eric Clapton is one of the towering figures of contemporary music. His work with the Yardbirds, John Mayall, Cream, and Blind Faith alone would have been enough to guarantee his place in rock 'n' roll history, but that was only the beginning. His first solo album came out in 1970, and remains a staple on FM rock stations nearly thirty years later. After beating a drug addiction that threatened his life and career, Clapton found his true solo voice on the 1974 collection *461 Ocean Boulevard*. This first post-rehab project was a breezy album recorded at Criteria studios in Miami. It revealed a looser, more confident Clapton dabbling in reggae ("I Shot the Sheriff"), or straight ahead rock 'n' roll ("Mainline Florida"). His spiritual side was represented as well in the almost prayerful "Let It Grow," which begins with a direct reference to his signature song, the Robert Johnson blues classic "Crossroads."

Reflection

Have you ever been in a dilemma or a crisis, desperately seeking a solution when, in fact, a part of you already knows the answers, even though the rest of you cannot or will not see it? You know you should seek reconciliation with someone, but you are reluctant to do so. You have been telling your family and friends that you want to find a new job but after three months of talking you have not made a move. You want to deepen your relationship with your lover and make a real commitment but somehow the words escape you. You want to spend more time with your children, but you are so busy that the time just seems to pass by.

You are, like Eric Clapton, "standing at the crossroads, trying to read the signs," when all the time the deepest and truest part of you already knows the answer. Indeed, "love is lovely," and in each of the situations mentioned above, and in virtually any other you can imagine, the clue is to "plant your love and let it grow."

If this is so, if a growth in our ability to love ourselves and others will take us from the crossroads and onto the right path, why is it so hard? Why do we have so much angst, so much indecision if we already know the basic answer? Perhaps it is because we are looking for an easier answer, a quicker, more painless fix. Society constantly tells us that it exists and that we deserve it. There is no need to listen to that intuitive voice within that is calling you to dig deeper for a solution with all of the hard work and sacrifice that may entail. Go for the surface solution and keep right on chuggin' along.

No! Every time you reach one of those crucial crossroads "plant your love and let it grow" and you will be given what you need. (Author's note: We know this works because we have tried it. We also know how hard it is to live on that level of trust. We struggle with it every day.)

Actions

▲ Are you presently in a difficult situation, looking for the right answer? Should you do this or that, go one way or the other? Ask yourself whether there is another level to the question on which you already know the answer. If so, try to spend some quiet time getting in touch with that answer and what it may mean for your life.

▲ Try to help someone in a similar dilemma to see the deeper level of the answer.

▲ Reflect on Eric Clapton's line "plant your love and let it grow." Is there a situation that stands out for you in which you have done precisely that and it made a major positive difference? If so, find an appropriate way to celebrate it. Is there another unresolved situation for which that line is the ultimate answer? How can you start planting? What is the first step?

Album

Crossroads; Eric Clapton; Polydor 835 261-2.

LYIN' EYES
▲ *(Henley/Frey)* ▲
The Eagles

Background

They were one of the biggest success stories of the seventies. From Linda Ronstadt's former backup group to the premiere exponents of rock 'n' roll Southern California style, the Eagles landed on the charts in 1972 and stayed there until their premature (and, thankfully, not permanent) dissolution in 1980. Core members Glenn Frey and Don Henley were there through it all. As songwriters and vocalists, their bittersweet examinations of the modern day California lifestyle provided a revealing counterpoint to the more idealistic musings of fellow West Coast troubadours, the Beach Boys. Their country-flavored yet oh-so-sophisticated rock 'n' roll took hard looks at all aspects of ill-fated male/female relationships from cheatin' hearts to lyin' eyes.

Reflection

You can hide lying eyes, but only for a while. The eyes are the mirrors of the soul and, eventually, they betray its dark secrets. That's why it is so important to be able to look someone in the eye and believe what that person is saying. When there is deep eye presence, souls are open to each other and the possibility of deceit, while still there, is minimal. It is when people lose their gaze for each other that deep trouble begins. The lies may be about sexual infidelity but they are not limited to this one area of deception. They may be about an addiction or an obsession or some other dimension of infidelity or distancing that is too shameful or painful to express. Eventually, though, the eyes have it. They are the giveaway.

    The eye contact in both your personal and business relationships is crucial to the level of mutual understanding and trust. If you look at someone with whom you are about to undertake an important business transaction and what you get back is a blank stare or a constantly diverted look, be careful. It may simply be shyness, but it may also be a cover for deceit. If you are trying to establish intimacy with a friend, family member, or lover and the other person constantly avoids your eyes, it may be protective shyness or tiredness, but it may also be the sign of a deep hurt from the past or in the present that is blocking you from sight. If your words, the tone of your voice, and your body language are all accepting and inviting rather than nosy or judgmental, you may be able to penetrate beyond the eye wall, and catch a glimpse of the beauty and truth that is within.

Actions

▲ Do you find it hard to maintain eye contact with people? If so, be conscious of it and try it a little bit at a time in situations that are less threatening.

▲ If there are particular people with whom you find it difficult to make eye contact, ask yourself why. Are you trying to hide something from them or are you trying to hide a part of yourself? Is there something you don't trust about them?

▲ Is there someone you care about who has trouble making eye contact with you? If you feel comfortable doing it, gently mention the problem and see how the person responds.

▲ When you sense that someone has lying eyes how do you handle the situation? Do you confront or do you keep the information in mind and wait for the appropriate time to see if it is accurate?

Album

One of These Nights; the Eagles; Asylum 7E-1039-2.

MY HOMETOWN
▲ *(Springsteen)* ▲
Bruce Springsteen

Background

It is one of the great paradoxes of the pursuit of fame. Working-class kids reach for the stars with a guitar and a sackful of songs. Most don't make it, and retreat to more conventional ways of making a living, but a precious few grab the brass ring and attain vast amounts of wealth and fame. The money and the notoriety take them light years away from their humble roots. It becomes increasingly difficult to write about the poor and misfortunate as you enjoy the fruits and luxuries of enormous success. There are exceptions, of course. Harry Chapin was one. Bruce Springsteen is another. Throughout his amazing rise to the zenith of modern rock stardom, Bruce has retained his empathy and sensitivity to the plight of the downtrodden. "My Hometown" on *Born in the U.S.A.* is a perfect example.

Reflection

Before this century most Americans grew up, lived, and died in their hometowns. Now, most of us move at least once or twice during our childhoods and we are long gone from our hometowns right after high school or college. For some of us, our hometown is a nice place to go back for a family visit, if our parents haven't retired elsewhere. For some, it has radically changed, as in Bruce Springsteen's song, and we feel we can't go back. For still others there is no hometown, only steps along the way.

Neither of us lives in our hometown any longer, but we have fond memories—and some not so fond. Each of us has raised our children in a single town and both of those towns were better than those of our youth. Our children have all thanked us and have felt a kind of security and comfort about their hometowns. The oldest have already started moving away, but they still have a loyalty to their hometowns. We suspect that they will be very careful about choosing a hometown for their children.

There is another quality about many Americans that is very much in tension with the strong American desire for a hometown. It is that frontier spirit that says if it is not working for you in one place, pack up and move on to a better place. We do it in U-Hauls rather than in covered wagons, but the result is the same. These two powerful, seemingly conflicting myths of hometown and mobility can lead to a listless kind of rootlessness. Some of us secretly mourn the connectedness of our hometowns, and will try desperately to find it again. Others of us never knew it because we moved so many times as children, and yet there is something in each of us that longs for that feeling of home.

Actions

▲ Do you have any nostalgia about your hometown, any desire to go back again? Have you done it? How did it work out? If not, what's keeping you?

▲ If your hometown was a negative experience for you, for whatever reason, what have you done to expel the bad memories? Maybe it means going back and confronting something or someone. More probably, it means coming to some kind of closure about past fears, betrayals, or failures. How might you reach that closure?

▲ Are you in a new adult hometown or neighborhood, or are you still moving from place to place because of job transfers, family needs, or your own desire for change? What kind of hometown or urban neighborhood would be right for you? If it is the one you are in now, what makes it so good and how are you involved in your community? If you haven't found it yet, where should you be looking?

Album

Born in the USA; Bruce Springsteen; Columbia CK 38653.

MY PRAYER

▲ *(Kennedy/Boulanger)* ▲

The Platters

Background

The Platters were one of the greatest vocal groups of the fifties and sixties with many top-forty hits to their credit. They were, in fact, the first black group to have a number-one single on the pop charts with "My Prayer" in August of 1956. It was originally a French song by Georges Boulanger entitled "Avant de Mourir." Songwriter Jimmy Kennedy wrote English lyrics for it in the late thirties and retitled it "My Prayer." Seventeen years later, it was offered to the Platters as the followup to "The Great Pretender." In the year of Elvis it stayed at the top of the charts for two weeks, between two Presley classics, "I Want You, I Need You, I Love You" and "Hound Dog."

Reflection

"My Prayer" is a love song through and through, but it still serves as an excellent prism through which to look at the many facets of prayer. According to a recent survey, 78 percent of Americans believe in the power of prayer. This is very good news in such a secular age. There are many and varied types of prayer: group and individual, public and private, formal and informal. There are prayers of praise and thanksgiving, prayers of healing and petition for oneself or for others, prayers of repentance and sorrow, prayers of forgiveness and joy, and so on.

For many people, prayer is more like bargaining. You know, "Hey God, if you do such and such, I'll do such and such." Or rather, "If you do such and such, I'll *never* do such and such again!" That's not prayer, that's *Let's Make a Deal*. It's not the way it works, of course. The best definition of prayer is still, simply, talking to God. How you do it, where you do it, when you do it is completely up to you. But we'll tell you this, the more you do it, the better it goes. Practice makes perfect, after all.

One final thought about prayer. Would it surprise you to discover how many rock 'n' roll songs are really prayers in disguise? You'll meet a good number of them in the pages of this book—"Don't Let Me Be Misunderstood," "Forever Young," "Let It Grow," "Spirit in the Sky," to name a few. You see, contrary to the old stereotype, there's plenty of good news in rock 'n' roll. And that's the gospel truth!

*A*ctions

▲ Do you believe in the power of prayer or is it something foreign to you? Is prayer a regular part of your life or do you pray only when you are in deep trouble? Are you still caught in the let's make a deal prayer trap or have you gotten past that one?

▲ One of the best clues we have ever heard about prayer is that it doesn't change God's mind, but it may change our minds, and hearts. It helps us to connect with the deepest and best parts of ourselves, the spirit within us and all around us. Once that connection is made and maintained over a period of time something emerges within us. Sometimes it is a long sought answer, guidance in a problem. At other times, it is an undiscovered self or a long-lost part of ourselves from a better time. Prayer can help us to know who we are, where we are going, and most important, that we are not alone. But none of that will happen unless we try and try again, when no instant magic solution emerges.

*A*lbum

Golden Hits; The Platters; Mercury 826 447.

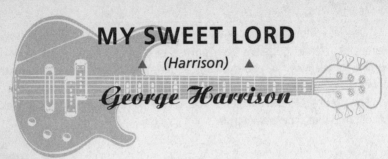

MY SWEET LORD
▲ (Harrison) ▲
George Harrison

Background

We have already noted how George Harrison exploded in a songwriting frenzy after the breakup of the Beatles. Many of his compositions reflected a growing interest in, and curiosity about, religion and spirituality. The roots of these inclinations can certainly be traced back to his Beatle days in songs such as "Within You, Without You" and "The Inner Light." They can also be traced back to George's connection to Indian music, culture, and mysticism. He gave free rein to these interests through his solo career. On *All Things Must Pass* alone, you will find deeply religious explorations in the title song, "What Is Life," "The Art of Dying," "Hear Me Lord," and, of course, the first single from this three-record set, which went right to number one all over the world in the winter of 1970–71, "My Sweet Lord."

Reflection

Every once in a while, you are aware that something is missing in your life, so you try to figure out what it is and then find it. It may be some form of wealth, power, success, or more of any of the above. When you have achieved these material goals, though, you will still have that yearning for more. Hopefully, you see that more of any of these things will continue to leave you empty and only push you toward getting more and more. You realize you need to switch gears and find your meaning in love, friendship, family, creativity, and service to others. No more superficial materialism for you! No more being driven to pile up one success after the other. You have finally found peace and happiness.

Congratulations! You are living your life well, exercising your creativity; giving, not just getting; and enjoying the wonder of deep relationships. Still, every once in while, you have a tinge of that old feeling of unfulfillment, of emptiness, a strange sense of being out of place.

St. Augustine named it when he said "Our hearts are restless, until they rest in thee." That's what George Harrison is singing about. At the height of his musical and economic success, he immersed himself into Hindu spirituality and had enough experience of a mystical presence that he wanted more. That's what we all want, community with each other and with God or whatever name we might give to a higher power.

*A*ctions

▲ Do you often feel like you are in a spiritual desert, wandering aimlessly, thirsting for something more?

▲ Is there any form of spirituality in your life? Do you go to church or temple, but still experience nothing on a spiritual level? Have you grown away from your religion, and now have no spiritual tradition?

▲ There is hunger for spirituality in our age that leads people into cults, superficial new-age fads, various forms of true believer, "I'm right, you're wrong" fundamentalism, and often into wonderful soul-enlivening experiences. Have you found yours yet? It may be in the spiritual or mystical dimensions of traditional Judeo-Christian religions, in eastern or native spirituality or in some combination of many streams of spirituality that have watered your previous spiritual experience. Don't be discouraged. The longing will always be there but the quest for fulfillment is its own reward.

*A*lbum

All Things Must Pass; George Harrison; Capitol CDP 7 46688 2.

NATURE'S WAY
▲ (California) ▲
Spirit

Background

There are a number of very stark and telling differences between the rock 'n' roll of the fifties and the rock 'n' roll of the sixties. For one thing, music of the latter decade dealt with many social and political issues. No subject was considered to be beyond the scope of the new breed of songwriter/musicians. Teen laments about love lost and found were supplanted by weighty explorations of every subject imaginable—sex, death, war, peace, religion, and ecology all became fodder for the ambitious, uninhibited songwriters of the sixties. The struggle to protect the environment in particular gave birth to a number of ecological anthems including "What Have They Done to the Rain" by Malvina Reynolds, "Whose Garden Was This" by Tom Paxton, "Earth Anthem" by the Turtles, and, one of the best, "Nature's Way" by the Los-Angeles–based group, Spirit.

Reflection

Nature does have a way of telling us when something is wrong, whether it is a pain in some part of our body or a cosmic pain that lets us know something is wrong with our planet. Most of us find it hard to listen to our bodies when they give us early warning signs that something is out of whack. Usually, we wait until the pain becomes stronger and more frequent. Sometimes we wait too long and there is serious damage.

There are all sorts of warning signs of environmental destruction, beginning with the ever-increasing global warming, huge holes in the ozone layer over the North and South Poles, the rampant destruction of the rainforests, and the virtual disappearance of the once-massive Aral Sea in the former Soviet Union and Lake Chad in Africa. Coming dangerously close to home, we face increasing rates of breast cancer in women, dramatically decreasing rates of fertility in men and the growing *circle of poison:* pesticides manufactured in the United States, used on Third-World crops, and then consumed back here by millions of unsuspecting Americans.

Many of our leaders tell us not to worry about any of these dangers when our life expectancy is increasing, medical science is advancing, and the power to change anything is far beyond us. However, the root cause of our powerlessness is our disconnection with nature. Just as we often become cut off from our own bodies because we have failed to honor, respect, and take care of them, so too, when we see nature as a series of objects provided for our use and exploitation we can find ourselves alienated from the very life systems that sustain us: the air that we breathe, the water that we drink, and the land that provides our food and is our home.

*A*ctions

▲ Have you been missing any of nature's warning signs about your bodily health: Are you frequently feeling tired, do you cough every day but keep right on smoking, are you overweight, do you work or live in a stressful environment?

▲ Think about your bodily health, and determine one action you should take and one thing you should stop doing to improve your health.

▲ There are dozens of environmental causes, and hundreds of things you can do to help protect or renew the earth. Check out the work of several environmental groups and choose one for further study and potential volunteer work. At the same time, figure out one action you can take on a regular basis that will help in some small way to preserve our planet, such as recycling or cleaning up a park or beach. As you do it, feel in solidarity with the millions of your fellow humans who are performing similar healing actions.

*A*lbum

Time Circle; Spirit; Epic/Legacy E2K 47363.

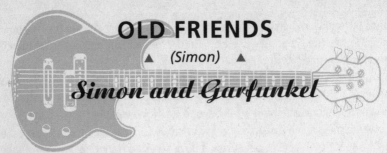

OLD FRIENDS

▲ *(Simon)* ▲

Simon and Garfunkel

Background

As a public service, we would like to alert you to two rock 'n' roll media events of the future. Remember, you read it here first! Event number one will take place on June 18, 2006. That is the day when Paul McCartney will celebrate his sixty-fourth birthday. Why is that significant? "Will you still need me, will you still feed me, when I'm sixty-four?" Event number two will occur between November of 2011 and October of 2012. Sometime during that year, destiny dictates that Paul Simon and Art Garfunkel will share a park bench together somewhere on this planet—preferably Queens, New York. That's when these two old friends will reach the milestone predicted on their 1968 album *Bookends*. Or, to put it another way, "How terribly strange to be seventy!"

Reflection

Old friends know parts of your life that you may have forgotten. Even when you haven't seen them in a long time, you can resume your relationship as though you were with them yesterday. They are the bedrock of your life. They help you know who you are.

Tragically, in our fast-paced, transient society, there are millions of people who do not have old friends anymore. They have moved away, lost touch, or been disconnected by a series of petty misunderstandings, jealousies, or hurts. There are acquaintances, business associates and partners, playmates on the tennis court, the golf course, or in the gym, some of whom could become friends, but there are no real long-term friends.

Value your friends, especially the old friends. Treasure them, work on the relationship, celebrate them, sacrifice for them, and hope for as much in return. Do not be surprised, however, when things don't work out quite that way. There are inequalities in all relationships: areas of great strengths and glaring weaknesses, disappointments, betrayals, and, hopefully, forgiveness.

Underneath all of this there is the core of the old friendship, a place where you and your friend meet and are bonded continually. It is a comfortable place, a nourishing place, a necessary place for you to have in your life. If you have it, realize how important it is for you, cherish it, and nurture it. If no such relationship exists for you, do not despair. It is never too late. A friend you make now can be your old friend twenty years later.

*A*ctions

▲ Do not take old friends for granted. Make that extra phone call, write a card or letter, or send that e-mail! Better still, develop ways to maintain and rejuvenate your friendship: special times together, rituals you share, or a common task or project.

▲ If there is an old friend you still care about but who is not in your life, make contact again. If there was a rift of some sort, try to build a reconciliation.

▲ Evaluate yourself as a friend. Congratulate yourself on your fidelity and caring in your friendships. Be honest with yourself about how you can be a better friend, despite all the constraints on your time and resources.

*A*lbum

Bookends; Simon and Garfunkel; Columbia CK9529

OUR HOUSE

▲ *(Nash)* ▲

Crosby, Stills, Nash and Young

Background

So who's the most hopelessly romantic member of Crosby, Stills and Nash? That's an easy one. It's always been Graham Nash who has softened the group's rougher edges with his gentle, contemplative ballads about life, love, and the human condition. Not that he isn't capable of rocking out with the best of them, it's just that his soft songs and soft voice have always spoken the loudest. "Lady of the Island," "Teach Your Children," "Just A Song Before I Go," and especially "Our House," have taken up a permanent residence in our hearts. Need proof? There's a wonderful moment in the *No Nukes* movie when Graham turns over the chorus of "Our House" to the audience at Madison Square Garden. The response is thunderous and overwhelming. The single version of "Our House" made it to number thirty on the U.S. charts in October 1970.

Reflection

There are an awful lot of great rock n roll songs about going home (see "Homeward Bound," p. 90 and "My Hometown," p. 128). But what happens once you get there? Is your home merely a place to eat, sleep, and take showers, or is it more than that? Ideally, it is your true refuge, your one special place that offers shelter, comfort, and peace. It's the one place you return to again and again to refuel and recharge, to spend quality time with your significant others, to create and re-create.

Unfortunately, we live in such a fast-paced society today that we've gotten away from the idea of a home base that shelters us for long periods of our lives. In another age, it was much more common for the family compound to serve several generations. It was also possible for a person to be born, grow up, get married, raise a family, and die in the same house. That sense of continuity, familiarity, and interconnectedness all too often gets lost in our modern-day mobile society.

Our culture abounds with adages about our primary dwelling place: "Home Is Where the Heart Is," "A Man's Home Is His Castle," "Home Sweet Home," "Wherever I Hang My Hat Is Home," and, the ever popular, "A House Is Not a Home." It's this last one that Graham Nash reinvents in his song "Our House." He celebrates the simplest trappings of a happy home— pets in the yard, flowers in a vase, a roaring blaze in the fireplace—but he in- fuses these accessories with the most essential ingredient of all that makes this house a home. And that is a sharing, loving couple who give all of these things true meaning. In that spirit, let's close this reflection with one final dwelling place adage: "There's No Place Like Home!"

Actions

▲ Do you consider your house or apartment to be a true home? If not, what can you do to make it a more comfortable refuge? What is miss- ing, and how can you provide it?

▲ Do you thank the other members of your family or your roommates for what they do to make your house a home, or do you take them for granted much of the time?

▲ The interpersonal, emotional, and spiritual tone of your home is even more important than the physical. Is there something you can do to im- prove it?

Album

Déjà Vu; Crosby, Stills, Nash and Young; Atlantic SD 19118-2.

PEOPLE GOT TO BE FREE
▲ (Cavaliere/Brigati) ▲
The Rascals

Background

The young Rascals had their roots in Joey Dee's Starlighters of "Peppermint Twist" fame. Felix Cavaliere, Eddie Brigati, and Gene Cornish formed their own group in 1965, with the addition of Dino Danelli on drums. Their first two hits were cover versions of other people's songs, but, inspired by the Beatles, Cavaliere and Brigati were soon writing their own hits such as "Lonely Too Long," "How Can I Be Sure," and "Groovin'." Most of these were love songs. But, in 1968, devastated by the assassinations of Martin Luther King and Bobby Kennedy, Cavaliere and Brigati poured their hearts out in the overtly political "People Got to Be Free." Their record-company executives were a little nervous about tampering with a successful formula, but they needn't have worried. The song soared to number one in August 1968 and stayed there for five straight weeks.

Reflection

More than half the people in our world do not have the basic freedoms that we take for granted, but as we go about our everyday lives exercising those freedoms, it is all too easy to forget about their plight. Here are just a few of the faces without freedom. There are no pictures in this book, but let your imagination take over and see their faces, feel the pain in their eyes.

The greatest destroyer of freedom is war. Although, at the time of this writing, there are no international wars raging, there are internal, often undeclared, wars going on in Afghanistan, Sudan, Central African Republic, Cambodia, Burma, East Timor, Burundi, Kashmir, Palestine, Uzbekistan, Colombia, Sierra Leone, Kurdistan, Liberia, Somalia, Northern Ireland, Rwanda, Egypt, and Chechnya, and doubtless more by the time you read this. The people who lose their freedom are mostly unarmed civilians who live in fear of the knock on the door, the attack in the middle of the night, or the tens of millions of live, unexploded land mines that kill 26,000 people a year that may be in their fields or forests. They are also the 43 million people forced from their homes who live in camps or wander from place to place.

The faces without freedom also include millions more who are living as virtual slaves, many of them children sold by their parents into servitude to help feed the rest of the family. There are a billion more, yes, that's right, one billion, who are so poor and malnourished that their lives could hardly be called free. Theirs are the faces of hunger and disease and abject poverty, sometimes in the midst of plenty.

Lest we be consumed by despair from all these faces of unfreedom, know that they are not mere passive victims. Most are struggling against great odds to gain their freedom and to maintain their dignity. They ask not for our pity, but for whatever support and solidarity we can give them, through out presence, our protest, and our prayers.

Actions

▲ Do not be afraid to know about the faces of *unfreedom*. They will disturb you, but they may also awaken and enrich your life if you let them. You can begin by learning more about the places in the world where freedom is minimized or threatened by war, political, social, religious, or economic oppression, or by slavery.

▲ Each day take a moment to remember the faces of unfreedom and talk about them with your family and friends.

▲ Contact a human rights group or international hunger and poverty agency, and find out how you can help.

▲ Become more aware of the dangers to freedom right here in the United States, especially the lack of freedom for people who suffer from spouse or child abuse, discrimination of any kind, or economic injustice. Join a group that is working to preserve these freedoms right here at home.

Album

Anthology; The Rascals; Rhino R2 71031.

PRESENCE OF THE LORD
▲ *(Clapton)* ▲

Blind Faith

Background

It was one of the shortest-lived supergroups in the history of rock 'n' roll—one album, one tour, then gone forever. That's the story of Blind Faith, the superstar quartet that took off like a rocket then fell back to earth in tatters, all within a few months. Back in 1969, Eric Clapton was still searching for the best vehicle for his talents after stints with the Yardbirds, John Mayall, and Cream. He joined forces with rock 'n' roll wunderkind Steve Winwood, on the loose following the first of many departures from Traffic. Rick Grech from Family was recruited on bass, and Ginger Baker, another Cream veteran, was added on drums. The restless members soon moved on to other pursuits, but they left behind an album full of great songs and performances, including Clapton's memorable and moving "Presence of the Lord."

Reflection

Every one of us, including Eric Clapton, is looking for a way to live. Clapton says he has finally found it, in the presence of the Lord. He might also be the first to agree that it is most elusive. There are so many distractions, so many competitors, so many temptations. How do you stay in the presence of the Lord throughout any busy day? At any given moment, you are bombarded by questions, demands, requests, and information from family, friends, and co-workers, to say nothing of the barrage of sound and sight from the media. At any given time, you can feel totally disconnected from the presence, precisely because you are mindlessly and spiritlessly connected for a few seconds or minutes to hundreds of other impulses within a brief period of time. It is as though you were floating in an endless pinball game, bouncing off one bumper after another, hearing all those bells ring at the same time but winning no prize, finding no safe haven.

Then, suddenly, you find it once again, in the eyes of someone you love or someone in need, in the smile of a child or the flight of a bird, in the delight of swimming in a cool lake, feeling the warmth of the sun, or seeing that same sun quietly slip off the horizon, leaving behind evershifting masterpieces of radiant color. Or, you may rediscover the presence of the Lord in conflict and pain, in desperate longing or need. But then, just when you can say with Eric Clapton that you have finally found it, it slips away and you feel lost again, frustrated that what seemed powerful and permanent is now teasingly beyond reach. The secret, of course, is that the presence never leaves, only we do. The hope is that we can always come back.

Actions

▲ The term Lord means different things to different people: Yahweh, God the Father, Jesus, Krishna, Buddha, and so on. It can also have a negative connotation of a distant but demanding deity who is judgmental and punishing. Who would want to live in that presence? Ask yourself whether there is still some of that mean-spirited fearsome God in you.

▲ The God who should have been taught to us as children and whose presence we should seek is a loving, healing, challenging, and supportive Lord. That's the presence to find and to share, but how? Seek no further, it is already there, within you and all around you.

▲ How do you try to open yourself to the presence of the Lord: prayer, meditation, going to church or temple, communing with nature, loving and helping others, especially those in need?

▲ No matter what you do, how hard you try, there will always be times when the presence seems very far away. Be patient, stay open, it will reappear in ways and at times you least expect.

Album

Crossroads; Eric Clapton; Polydor 835 261-2.

PRESSURE
▲ *(Joel)* ▲
Billy Joel

Background

As good a songwriter as Billy Joel is, he has often expressed his discomfort with the writing process. To hear him tell it, it's the hardest part of his job, the part he likes the least. So, back in 1982, when it came time to write songs for the album called *The Nylon Curtain*, Billy found himself in the familiar situation of staring at an empty music sheet pondering how to fill it. His secretary at the time noticed his furrowed brow, and said, "You look like you're under a lot of pressure. Why don't you write about that?" To his credit, Billy took the advice and knocked out one of the best songs on the album. Pressure? No sweat!

Reflection

The bills pile up. Your boss tells you to, "Do this, and do it now." Your spouse and your kids compete for every precious second of your time and attention, and your aging parent depends on you for support in the midst of a debilitating illness. Your head pounds, your stomach growls, and your heart races. Is this any way to live your life? You know it isn't, but you feel trapped by pressure, coming at you from all sides as in Billy Joel's song. Is there no escape from what seems like an ever-increasing avalanche of pressure?

Let's look for the solution first within yourself. How much of the pressure is really coming at you from the outside, and how much are you creating from the inside by your attitude and the way you deal with everyday life? Do you see yourself as an oppressed victim with few choices? Are you afraid to take chances and to stand up to some of the sources of pressure? Do you create your own worst pressure through procrastination and the inability to make decisions? If the answer is even a partial yes to any of these questions, you have a good clue to both the cause of and solution to your pressure.

There are many pressures that you definitely do not cause, but which you can influence and often control by a combination of relaxation techniques, exercise, a good sense of humor, someone who is supportive, and your own attitude.

Some people thrive on pressure. Most of us try to simply survive and, ultimately, that comes down to an attitude that sees things in perspective and does not allow troubles to be more than they really are.

*A*ctions

▲ Do you constantly feel pressure at work and/or at home? Have you identified the sources of the pressure and faced them or are you still avoiding them?

▲ If there is one major source of pressure, focus on what you can do either to eliminate it or deal with it. If there are multiple sources, pick one or two that you can actually change and begin there.

▲ What needs to change within you to help you deal better with pressure? Have you lost some of your sense of humor? Are you usually down on yourself? Have you stopped believing in yourself or your abilities? All of these self-putdowns can drain the energy you need to deal effectively with the everyday pressures of life. If you can change your attitude you may find that you have a whole different relationship to pressure.

*A*lbum

The Nylon Curtain; Billy Joel; CBS CK 38200.

PUT A LITTLE LOVE IN YOUR HEART
(DeShannon/Holiday/Myers)
Jackie DeShannon

*B*ackground

In a musical form dominated by men, Jackie DeShannon stands out as a woman singer/songwriter who has enjoyed a remarkably long and fruitful career. Her first taste of success came in the early sixties as a songwriter for "Little Miss Dynamite"—Brenda Lee. As the decade progressed, so did Jackie. She wrote "When You Walk in the Room," a top-forty hit for The Searchers in 1964 (which Bruce Springsteen frequently performed in concert in the seventies). She had a top-ten hit herself in 1965 with Hal David and Burt Bacharach's "What the World Needs Now Is Love." The message of that song influenced one of her own best-known songs which became a number-four single in the summer of 1969—"Put a Little Love in Your Heart."

*R*eflection

The late singer and humanitarian Harry Chapin was our friend and partner. We remember him saying over and over how he wanted desperately to make a difference in his life. His mottoes were "When in doubt, do something" and "You can make a difference." He passionately believed that one person could make a difference, and if several people of like mind and like heart got together they could make a major difference in society.

Where does it all start? The title of this song is not a bad place. The world will be a better place if you put a little love in your heart. You may not see the benefit right away, but you can begin to see it within yourself. Others can as well. They can feel it in your attitudes and approach to people. They can hear it in your words and in your tonality (another one of Harry's favorite terms). They can see it in your eyes and your smile. Eventually, they can experience it in the deeds you do which flow from the love in your heart.

Has the love in your heart been crushed or chased out by abuse, betrayal, disappointment, tragedy, depression, or sheer boredom? If so, put some back in every day. Where will you find it? Open your eyes and, more important, open your heart. It is all around you, dancing enticingly to catch your attention amidst all the dreariness and busyness that is also a part of your everyday life. If you look very carefully, you will also find that it is still alive inside you waiting to be invited once again to the dance.

*A*ctions

▲ What are the situations in your family, social, and business life in which you need to put a little love in your heart? Why is it difficult for you to do it? Try to identify what is preventing you from doing it and how you can overcome the obstacles.

▲ Sometimes it is not a question of big problems, but rather inattention, a lack of loving focus, or forgetting to pay attention to someone in the midst of a busy schedule.

▲ Identify one or two persons that you need to love more. How can you begin? Try to imagine yourself actually doing it.

▲ Remember some instances when you have put a little love in your heart, acted on it, and had good results. Sure, there are times when it backfires, but stay focused on the successes and allow them to encourage you to go further.

*A*lbum

The Very Best of Jackie DeShannon; Jackie DeShannon; United Artists UA-LA434-E.

REACH OUT I'LL BE THERE

▲ *(Holland/Dozier/Holland)* ▲

The Four Tops

Background

It wasn't called Hitsville, USA for nothing. The influence of Detroit-based Motown on the music of the world is inestimable. It was a sound, a style, and a rhythm that proved to be irresistible. The vision belonged to Berry Gordy Jr., who assembled one of the most creative and prolific talent rosters in the history of recorded music. The Temptations, the Supremes, the Miracles, Marvin Gaye, and Stevie Wonder represent just the tip of the iceberg of this musical empire. Another cornerstone of the company? The amazing Four Tops who scored a lengthy string of top-forty hits for Motown, including the number one single "Reach Out I'll Be There" in October of 1966.

Reflection

The title of this four-decade-old song contains one the most comforting messages any one of us can hope to hear. Imagine actually having someone in your life who is there for you, at your call to comfort you in your suffering, advise you in difficult decisions, and love you for who you are, not who you should be. What a gift! What a treasure! If you have someone like that, it's time to celebrate.

Whoever this person is, never ever take him or her for granted. Is it your spouse, best friend, parent, sister, brother, or another? Whoever it is, show gratitude. Allow your love to flow freely to that person and, if possible, reciprocate the support. As is often the case, however, you may find that you cannot do all that you want to show your appreciation for this wonderful person. Keep trying, but don't try too hard. Accept the gift graciously. There may come a time when you can give some of it back to that person, but simply knowing that you are grateful may be enough for the moment. It may also be that you will be called to share the gift of support that you have received with some other person at a time of need. The key to all of this is in the first part of the title, "Reach Out." When you need help, and when you see someone in need, be willing to extend yourself. That very extension either way will help you to grow into the person you want to be.

*A*ctions

▲ Is there someone in your life who has been there for you and is still there? Is your reaction pure joy and gratitude, or is there a mixture of discomfort or even resentment? Try to sort out your feelings, so that you can show genuine gratitude without any tinges of diminishment or indebtedness. Of course, if the person who has helped you projects any dimension of condensation or control, be careful. The supportive presence may have come with a high price.

▲ Is there someone that you continually reach out to help? What kind of response have you gotten back? Is the relationship two-way? If not, is that because the other person does not have the capacity to be there for you at this time, or because you do not want that reciprocal kind of relationship? Your attitude may be quite appropriate for the situation, or it may be that you find it too difficult to accept help or even ask for it.

*A*lbum

Billboard Top Rock 'n' Roll Hits 1966; Various Artists; Rhino R2 70627.

REASON TO BELIEVE

▲ *(Hardin)* ▲

Tim Hardin

*B*ackground

Tim Hardin was a dark, brooding genius of sixties music. He became an influential figure first in Cambridge, Massachusetts, then in New York City, with his intriguing blend of blues, folk, and jazz coupled with poetic lyrics and smoky vocal intonations. He was a songwriter's songwriter. His own recordings sold modestly, and his greatest success came from cover versions of his best known songs such as "If I Were a Carpenter" by Bobby Darin, "Misty Roses" by the Youngbloods, and "Reason to Believe" by Rod Stewart. Unfortunately, Hardin died of a drug overdose at the age of thirty-nine, in December 1980.

*R*eflection

You've heard this story many times before. Perhaps you have even lived it in your own relationships or that of a friend. She dumped him, but he's still hanging in there, still hoping against hope, still looking to find a reason to believe, even though the situation is beyond belief for any rational person. This is not about reasonable people, though, it's about a man hopelessly, deliriously addicted to a love that is no more.

So, you ask yourself why would anyone put himself through that kind of torture? Until you are there. Only then can you begin to understand this kind of over-the-edge behavior. Tim Hardin says it well. A girl like her is worth it. Case closed.

When the love bug bites someone that hard, it is nearly impossible to talk that person out of the futile pursuit or the endless waiting. That's not to say you shouldn't try or that you should give up on your friend because there has been a temporary loss of the senses. On the contrary, it is at times like these that the presence and good sense of a good friend can make the difference between recovery and probable depression. It can get that crazy.

*A*ctions

▲ If you know someone in this situation, try to help your friend to realize that it is over, to mourn the death of the relationship and begin the healing process. The hardest part is if the person is consumed by guilt for having blown the relationship. "If only I had . . ." "If only I didn't . . ." Self-forgiveness is a long, hard road, but it is much easier to travel with friends.

▲ Anytime you have this kind of experience in your own life, try to remember similar experiences of loss. How did you help yourself then? What worked that might help now? Do you have someone to share the burden? What did you learn back then about yourself that might figure in the recovery now?

*A*lbums

Hang on to a Dream; Tim Hardin; Polydor 314 521 583-2. *Every Picture Tells a Story;* Rod Stewart; Mercury 822 385-2.

REFUGEE

▲ *(Petty/Campbell)* ▲

Tom Petty and the Heartbreakers

*B*ackground

Tom Petty and the Heartbreakers came along at the end of the seventies. The golden age of progressive rock was over. The disco craze was in full swing, and new wave and punk rock were the fads *du jour.* Unfortunately for Tom, his original record company promoted him to radio stations as another new-wave sensation. This was a complete disservice to Tom, as it soon became apparent that his undeniable talent owed less to new wave than it did to the glorious traditions of folk rock, the British Invasion, and mainstream southern rock 'n' roll. Hit after hit confirmed this, including the 1980 top-forty single "Refugee."

*R*eflection

There are 17 million people all over the world who are officially classified as refugees. Most are desperately poor, many living in camps that maintain them slightly above starvation level—sometimes. Still others are roaming from place to place, outside the law, outside the boundaries of normal society, always looking over their shoulder, always expecting the knock on the door in the middle of the night.

That is the spirit that haunts Tom Petty's song, the repeated cry that he does not want to be a refugee, not in the technical sense, but an emotional refugee in his own land, his own place. It is a protest song, not about the plight of international refugees but about the situation that most of us find ourselves in sometime in our lives. We feel that we are strangers in our own homes, aliens in our workplaces, refugees from a past life and homeland that once made sense, in which we fit safely.

What makes us refugees in our own lives? It may come from a disagreement with the predominant culture and values of our society. We feel left out, that we are always swimming upstream against a strong current of opinion. It can also come from a personal tragedy, such as the breakup of a marriage, the death or serious illness of a loved one, the loss of a job or a prolonged depression. The power of the song is in the strength and passion of its resolve to fight back, the refusal to be imprisoned by domination or cut adrift by disregard.

The next time you feel any of these various types of alienation, pop this one into the CD player and feel the power of protest.

*A*ctions

▲ Do you ever feel as though you are a refugee? In what part of your life do you fell that way? What are the sources of your alienation? Try to name them specifically. That is the first step to reducing their power over you. The second step is to allow yourself to feel the pain of being a refugee. If you continue to deny it or cover it up, the shroud will only become more pervasive, and you will actually begin to feel a perverse kind of comfort in it. Meanwhile, it is eating away your vitality and your will to fight back.

▲ Focus on the parts of your life in which you are more or less content and in control. Draw strength from them. Allow them to enhance your self-confidence, spill over into the refugee territory, and invite the refugee part of you to come home.

*A*lbum

Greatest Hits; Tom Petty and the Heartbreakers; MCA MCAD 10813.

RESPECT
▲ (Redding) ▲
Aretha Franklin

Background

Otis Redding was on his way to becoming one of the biggest stars in music at the time of his death in a plane crash in December 1967. Already a soul sensation, he had crossed over to a larger mass audience following his appearance at the Monterey International Pop Festival six months before the accident. His own recordings had appeared on the charts since 1965, but it was a cover version of one of his best songs that rocketed to number one in June 1967—"Respect" by the Queen of Soul herself, Aretha Franklin.

Reflection

You can demand momentary attention through anger. You can buy temporary allegiance with money. You have to *earn* respect, usually one step at a time, inch by inch. What has been won slowly, built over a long period of time can be lost easily in one moment of indecision or in one hasty or pressured bad decision. Usually though, respect is lost in the same way it is won, little by little, through a series of misunderstandings, inattention, passive-aggressive behavior, petty meanness, deceptions, and betrayals of trust.

The way to keep respect for someone is to stay focused on the core goodness in that person. Play to their strengths, not weaknesses, but do not put them on a pedestal. There is always a temptation to tear down what we have built up when it does not meet our unrealistic and unrealized expectations.

What about the flip side? How can you gain and keep the respect of others? The wisdom is the same. Stay focused on your strengths. Don't create unrealistic expectations. Recognize your weaknesses and try to deal with them without being obsessed by them. Know who you are and be true to yourself. Perhaps most important, admit when you are wrong and be willing to say you are sorry and make amends to the people whose respect you want to keep.

The key to this song, though, is that it is sung by Aretha Franklin, a black woman, traditionally one of the hardest working, least appreciated, and most abused and misunderstood groups of people in America. What she says she wants is what everyone of us wants and what everyone of us must give each other—respect.

*A*ctions

▲ Who are the people you most respect? Why? What is it about them that you respect?

▲ How about the people you least respect or don't respect at all, what is it about them that takes away your respect?

▲ What do you believe people most respect in you?

▲ Do you respect yourself? If so, great, you should! We all should. If not, why not?

▲ Is there anyone in particular with whom you have a "respect problem," either that you do not respect the other person or vice versa? What can you do to remedy the situation? Focus on a first step.

*A*lbum

The Very Best of Aretha Franklin, the 60s; Aretha Franklin; Rhino R271598.

RUNNING ON EMPTY

▲ *(Browne)* ▲

Jackson Browne

Background

Live rock 'n' roll albums have always been a tricky business. They are often no more than excuses to put out live versions of greatest hits. There are exceptions, of course. Sometimes a live album documents a truly memorable and historic moment in music history (Woodstock, the Concert for Bangladesh). Sometimes a live album captures road-tested versions of songs that are actually improvements over the original studio recordings. And, sometimes, a live album dares to showcase brand new music, warts and all, in front of an audience hearing the material for the very first time. Such an album was *Running on Empty* by Jackson Browne in 1977. The result? A critical smash and the biggest-selling collection of songs in Jackson's long and distinguished career.

Reflection

Back around the turn of the century, our grandparents and greatgrandparents worked fifty or sixty hours a week. Because of the efforts of labor unions and effective legislation, that number was reduced to forty hours a week for most Americans by 1950. There was talk about the thirty-five or even thirty hour week and longer vacations. Books and courses appeared about the uses of leisure time. The shorter workweek had become part of the American dream, along with owning a home and a car, and retiring at age sixty-five.

Now, almost fifty years later, it is a dream deferred, if not lost, in our lifetime. Most of us are working longer hours and often at more than one job. Sometimes we do it just to survive and provide the basics for our families. Often we do it for the money, to acquire bigger and better toys. There are those of us who prefer to work rather than be with our families, for all sorts of reasons, most of them bad.

There is a tendency in this manic madness either to fill up any empty space with worklike, regimented, pseudo-leisure activities ("I gotta go, I'm late for the gym") or veg out for endless hours in front of the tube, watching reruns of reruns.

This is truly running on empty. It is a self-inflicted blindness that depletes any kind of vision of a genuinely good life. You may feel trapped in your job and your total lifestyle, but are you really? There are choices you can make. The word *recreation* means re-create. You can take the time to recreate the best in you, to renew your energy, your relationships, and your spirit.

When a car runs on empty for too long, it stops and it won't go again until it is filled. Most of us will never let that happen to our cars. It's funny how we let it happen to ourselves.

*A*ctions

▲ Every one of us runs on empty at times. The real question is whether this has become a chronic condition for you. Be honest about it, and if you find yourself in that kind of situation all too often, then do something about it. Start by figuring out all the reasons why it is happening, and de-velop a plan for getting out of the pattern or at least slowing it down. Share your concerns with your spouse or a good friend and ask them to be your partner for change, to keep you to your plan. You may feel guilty and think you are neglecting you responsibilities when, of course, you are not. They can keep you straight on that one, and prevent you from being deterred by guilt.

▲ If someone you love is running on empty, offer to be a recreative part-ner to help ease the transition.

*A*lbum

Running on Empty; Jackson Browne; Asylum 6E 113-2.

RUNNING SCARED

▲ *(Orbison/Melson)* ▲

Roy Orbison

*B*ackground

He had one of the biggest voices in rock 'n' roll, and an overall talent to match. Roy Orbison began his career in great company. He was part of the original stable of artists at Sun Records in Memphis in the fifties that also included Johnny Cash, Jerry Lee Lewis, Carl Perkins, and Elvis Presley. Roy's early hits were very much rockabilly, but in the sixties he developed a style uniquely his own, centered around minipop melodramas with operatic overtones. The best of them were dark, moody, and full of dramatic tension. One of them, "Running Scared," became his first number-one single in June 1961.

*R*eflection

How can you ever know for sure? How long will those growing doubts eat away at you? Suppose the other person, the person who was your lover's lover before you, suddenly reappears and wants to resume the relationship? That's what Roy Orbison is obsessed with in this song. He captures the flavor of a fear that you may have experienced in your own life.

Some breakups are mean and ugly and final, some are clean and amicable, but final. There are others however, that are unresolved, leaving both parties haunted by what could have been. You go your separate ways but memories remain, passion that was shared is now unrequited. You enter a new relationship that begins to fill the void and, as time goes by, a new love, a more fulfilling and complete love, is born. Still, if the whole story of the lost love has been shared, including the intensity of the feelings and the extent of the sexual ardor, a seed of doubt may grow into a tangled garden of jealously. Although you may be totally faithful, beyond reproach, if your new lover suffers from a history of personal insecurity, even the normal disagreements in the ebb and flow of marital intimacy may be cause for suspicion. All of which leads to the notion that while honesty in usually a good policy in revealing past relationships, certain details and feelings are better left unspoken. Some relationships are better closed forever, despite the occasional quivers of the heart that may remain, lest they threaten what is now not mere fantasy, but heartfelt love.

$\mathcal{A}$ctions

▲ How do you deal with past loves in your present relationship? How much should you tell? How much do you really want to know? If you have said too much or know too much, how do you deal with it?

▲ It is so hard to determine the depth of revelation that is appropriate. What do you say about any of your past infidelities, especially if they led to the demise of the relationship? Do you fess up or quietly learn from your past mistakes?

▲ If you still feel strangely drawn to a past lover, although you know that it is over and you are glad that it is over, should you reveal your feelings? That one shouldn't be too hard to figure out.

▲ Honesty in a relationship is essential. Trust cannot be built on deception. Yet the past is the past and unless its effects endure into the present (as in this song) potential damage must be weighed carefully on both sides.

$\mathcal{A}$lbum

All Time Greatest Hits; Roy Orbison; Monument AGK 45116.

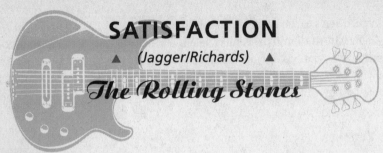

SATISFACTION
▲ *(Jagger/Richards)* ▲

The Rolling Stones

Background

The Beatles and the Rolling Stones are inextricably linked in the history of rock 'n' roll. In many ways, the Stones were the darker side of the Fab Four. The Beatles just wanted to "hold your hand," but the Stones wanted to "spend the night together." The Beatles wanted to "let it be," the Stones wanted to "let it bleed." After operating in the shadow of the Beatles in the early days of the British Invasion, the Stones finally came into their own with their 1965 anthem "Satisfaction," which went straight to number one on the U.S. charts in July and stayed there for four weeks.

Reflection

As Mick Jagger prances and stalks about the stage in his rock 'n' roll theater, he often has a message that goes against the grain but is right on. In this case it is his deftly sneering, cynical comments aimed at advertising and our consumer society, where people are judged by the products they buy.

Every day we are bombarded with hundreds of ad messages on TV, radio, and in print telling us we are dull, stupid, unsexy, flabby, smelly, scraggly, constipated, naive, incompetent, and somehow unhappy and incomplete without their product. It's enough to make even a strong, secure person (all seven of them) melt into a blubbery blob of insecurity, hopelessly outclassed by all those confident, gorgeous people who do use these products regularly. At least they say they do—for big bucks.

It is definitely a fantasy world and in our more reflective moments (we hope, like this one) we know it. We are not fooled. But, let's admit it, these moments are rare excursions into the world of quiet, without the media bombardment of endless hucksterism. Most of the time we absorb this stuff with absolutely no consciousness of what is happening. It is part of the air that we breathe, and it does not get us satisfaction for more than a brief moment of a mild consumer fix before we descend once again into the satisfactionless pit.

*A*ctions

▲ Think of several situations in which you said to yourself, "That's stupid. Who do they think they're kidding? That's one product I will not buy, because they are lying and they're insulting my intelligence." Come on now, you must remember a few that hit you that negatively. Did you stick to your guns?

▲ List some of the most useless or harmful products that you have seen or heard advertised. Think about how advertisers try to deceive you into buying them.

▲ Look around your home. Are there any items that you'd now consider nonessential purchases? What made you buy them? Were you swayed by advertising?

▲ Were you disappointed after you brought them home or much later? What disillusioned you?

▲ Are there any ways that you can become less dependent on unnecessary consumer items?

*A*lbum

Out of Our Heads; the Rolling Stones; ABKCO 74292.

SECRET O' LIFE
▲ *(Taylor)* ▲

James Taylor

Background

James Taylor has been part of our lives for three decades now. We know people who can chart all the major events of their lives according to the album that James had out at the time. Let's see, it goes something like this, "I was in college when *Sweet Baby James* came out; graduated in 1974 just after *Walking Man* was released; got married in 1977 to the tunes on *JT;* the twins were born when *Flag* came out, and Dad passed away in 1985 right around the time of *That's Why I'm Here.*" And so on. You see . . . James is right. The secret of life is enjoying the passing of time.

Reflection

Every once in a while, do you find yourself in that delightful time and space in which you are intensely yet peacefully connected to all that surrounds you? You are walking on the street and you actually see the faces of the people passing by, the architecture of the buildings, and what is in the store windows. You have walked by a hundred times before but never noticed. You are playing with a baby or a toddler and you are giving your full attention, not trying to read or watch TV. Gradually, you become aware of being deeply engaged with this marvelous little person. You celebrate a birthday or anniversary and let your mind wander back through the years to similar events. You note the passage of time, not with panic or sadness, but with a feeling of well-being.

This special time and space is easily stolen away. A sudden call or distraction, and you are lost again in the endless array of daily tasks and concerns. Remember, though, that this "spirit space" is yours for the asking. You can go there any day of your life and be nourished. When you were a child you were warned not to go there: "Stop that day dreaming," "Pay attention."

Now it's called *meditation* or *reflection,* and so it's okay. Now you know the secret of life, or at least part of it. So says James Taylor, who is singing better than ever, despite the passage of many dark times in his journey.

*A*ctions

▲ What is the secret of life for you? Do you feel you have attained it, or at least a piece of it?

▲ How are you aware of the passage of time? Do you celebrate the seasons, get excited at the buds on the trees in spring, and the last golden leaves of autumn? Do you see birthdays and anniversaries as landmarks on your journey or grim reminders of your mortality?

▲ Is there a *spirit space* for you, that place where time stands still and you are fully present to whomever and wherever you are? How do you find that space? When you do find it, do you allow yourself to go there or are you deterred by the tasks at hand or the still active voices from childhood that tell you to get busy again?

*A*lbum

JT; James Taylor; CBS CJ 34811.

SHE'S LEAVING HOME
▲ *(Lennon/McCartney)* ▲

The Beatles

Background

When did parents start liking the Beatles? For some, it happened during that very first appearance on *The Ed Sullivan Show*. For others, it was after the release of *A Hard Day's Night*. The glowing reviews brought droves of adults into movie theaters where they discovered what their children knew all along—the Beatles were delightful! If there were still any holdouts in 1967, the release of *Sgt. Pepper* dispelled any remaining doubts about whether or not the Beatles should be taken seriously. At the time, *Life* magazine ran an article with printed lyrics to a number of the album's incredible songs. Even parents who still didn't like loud rock 'n' roll music had to admit that the Beatles meant business. Their music had obviously matured and they were dealing with some serious, weighty issues. Nowhere was this more obvious than in the song "She's Leaving Home."

Reflection

At some time or other every one of us needs to leave home. Every year, millions of teens leave home under difficult or even tragic circumstances like the young woman in this song. Some find their way, most do not, at least not for a long time. Each year, many millions more young people leave home under positive circumstances for schools, the service, or a job. The physical leaving allows them to leave emotionally as well, to cut the cord, and gradually become independent people. It also creates the possibility of having an adult relationship with the very people who have treated them like kids all their lives because, until now, that's exactly what they have been, their kids. Now, they can come home again as adults.

Of course, this is much easier said than done. So many people never really leave home emotionally, either because they are afraid to leave the comfort of their parents' protection or because their parents are still holding on too tightly, or both. In-law jokes abound in our society, but when one or both parties in a couple are still under the thumb of their parents, it is no laughing matter. It is one of the quickest knockout punches for what could otherwise have been a good marriage.

How can we continue to love and respect our parents when we become adults, without allowing then to dominate our lives and our relationships? We have to leave home. That does not necessarily mean a painful rejection of our parents. It does mean profound change for both parents and children and that may seem, at times, like disloyalty or ingratitude. Even when we have successfully left home there will be times when our parents try to exercise their authority, either because of some problem of control within them or because they have a legitimate concern for our well-being. Sometimes, the line is not all that clear. The clue here is for us to stand firm without being belligerent, to listen to good advice without falling into the parent control trap, to be respectful without finding ourselves back home emotionally as kids again rather than adults.

*A*ctions

▲ Try to remember what it was like when you left home physically. Was it mostly a positive, hope-filled move, or was it very negative or even traumatic? What role did your parents play in your leaving? How did you feel about it at the time? How do you feel now?

▲ Do you feel that you have successfully left home emotionally? Are there any more steps that you need to take?

▲ Is there someone that you know who is having difficulty leaving home emotionally, especially your spouse or child? How can you help?

*A*lbum

Sgt. Pepper's Lonely Hearts Club Band; The Beatles; Parlophone CDP 7 46442 2.

SHOWER THE PEOPLE

▲ (Taylor) ▲

James Taylor

*B*ackground

For a brief moment in the early seventies, James Taylor stood at the epicenter of American popular music. His album *Sweet Baby James* ushered in the era of the singer-songwriter who dominated the charts and captivated the hearts of American record buyers. Taylor appeared on the cover of *Time* magazine as the symbol of this new movement in rock 'n' roll. The glare of the spotlight was especially blinding for such a shy, sensitive soul as James, but he plunged himself into his work and scored success after success with albums that included imaginative reworkings of great oldies as well as heartfelt originals. One of the best of these was "Shower the People" from his *In The Pocket* album. It was released as a single in 1976 and climbed to number twenty-two on the national charts.

*R*eflection

A long time ago, a friend told a story about his mother coming into her children's rooms late at night and kissing them. He said, "She loved us while we were asleep." She never expressed any affection for them at other times, only while they were sleeping. He was more affectionate with his children, but it was always a struggle because it was a totally new experience for him. Interestingly enough, his wife was almost old enough to be his mother.

James Taylor is right on target when he says we should "shower the people we love with love." All too often, we are reluctant to tell people how much we care about them or to show affection, even with those we love deeply. If it has not been part of our experience it is understandable that we have difficulty expressing feelings, but what a tragic loss! Everyone of us feels better when we are praised, thanked, appreciated, and hugged. It may be difficult at first to accept all these glorious gifts but gradually they will heal us, nurture us, restore us, and allow us to give back in kind. The image of showering people with love, pouring it upon them gleefully, without cost or condition or compensation is truly magnificent.

*A*ctions

▲ Has anyone ever really showered you with love? How did it feel? Try to remember that experience, live a little of it again.

▲ Have you ever showered others with love? What kind of response did you get. Surprise, elation, rejection, acceptance, thankfulness, or perhaps even a return shower? Try to remember that experience as well and experience the feelings again.

▲ What prevents you from accepting the showers of love that people offer to you? How can you begin to accept them?

▲ Who in your life would you like to shower with love? What's the first step? Think about it! Try it!

*A*lbum

Greatest Hits; James Taylor; Warner Brothers 3113-2.

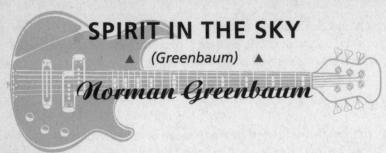

SPIRIT IN THE SKY

▲ *(Greenbaum)* ▲

Norman Greenbaum

*B*ackground

It's one of the great one-hit wonders of all time. Norman Greenbaum recorded "Spirit in the Sky" in 1970. It became an instant FM sensation and rose to number three on the top-forty charts as well. In the year of *Jesus Christ Superstar,* its overtly Christian message captured the ears of believers and nonbelievers alike. Besides, like most noteworthy rock 'n' roll, it had a great beat and you could dance to it! Almost thirty years later, "Spirit in the Sky" has enjoyed an exceptionally long shelf life. It is played constantly on oldies and classic-rock stations, and it keeps coming back as the background music for several commercials and on the soundtracks of many motion pictures—most recently *Apollo 13* and *Michael.* So, you see, there is an afterlife!

*R*eflection

Forget the mythical geographic references to "up" and "sky." Do you believe that when you die you will be welcomed by a benevolent spirit that has some presence with you now but will be totally present and totally accepting of you in the next life? You may call it the Holy Spirit, the Great Spirit, Mother Spirit, Father Spirit, the Spirit of Yahweh or Jehovah, the Spirit of Jesus, the Universal Spirit, or countless other names. All the names point to the same reality. A vast majority of the world's people believe there is a Spirit present with us in some kind of positive, protective way in this life and we will live with that Spirit in a new life after our death.

If that is the case, why do we have so much pain in this life and fear of death and the next life? There is a scientific principle called *entropy* that says that matter has a tendency to break apart, to disperse. That is also true on a mental and spiritual level. We learn things and then we forget them. We find a genuine closeness of spirit with friends, lovers, and families, and then it seems to slowly evaporate. We or they get drawn in different directions. It is similar to our relationship with the Spirit. The intensity comes and goes more often than we can imagine and when it is most distant we tend to have the most pain in life and fears of death.

Interestingly, the more we become influenced with the Spirit the more connected we become to the spirits of those around us and to the spirit of the earth, and the less we become burdened by the terrible fear of death.

Actions

▲ Do you believe in the presence of the Spirit in your life? What does that mean for you? What difference does it make?

▲ How do you become more open to the Spirit when you seem to be disconnected for a time? What are the places or experiences, who are the people that can help you to be reconnected to the Spirit?

▲ Try to remember the intensity of your feelings when you had peak Spirit experiences: in prayer or meditation, relationships, nature, creativity, and so on.

Album

Billboard Top Rock 'n' Roll Hits 1970; Various Artists; Rhino R2 70631.

STAND BY ME
▲ *(King/Glick)* ▲
Ben E. King

*B*ackground

The Drifters were among the great rhythm-and-blues performers of the fifties and sixties. But, like many groups of the era, their personnel kept changing almost from recording session to recording session. That's one of the reasons that they chose the name Drifters. Clyde McPhatter was the original lead singer, but more of their best-known hits came with Ben E. King as front man. King left the group in 1960 for a solo career and scored an immediate success with "Spanish Harlem," co-written and produced by Phil Spector. It was a song King wrote that became his biggest hit and his signature single in 1961—"Stand by Me." (The record became a top-ten hit all over again when it was used as the title song for the Rob Reiner motion picture of the same name.)

*R*eflection

"Stand by me! Don't run away! Don't let your hurt feelings or your anxieties or any of the stuff that is going on within you, no matter how important it may seem, take away your resolve to stand by me. Now is the time I need you. Now is the defining moment in our relationship, in my very life."

There are times when you might feel you want to say something like that to your mate, best friend, or a close relative. You know you are in deep trouble or crisis, and you can't handle it without help. There are other times when these words are far from your mind, when you are in a period of relative calm but somewhere down deep, you do feel that special person is standing by you. The resolve mentioned above has been tested before, again and again, in large and small matters, and been found strong. Those pleading words "stand by me" need not be said. It is mutually understood that the supportive presence is there, on call, at a moment's notice.

If you have even one person in your life like that, rejoice! If you are that person for someone, rejoice doubly! What a wonderful gift to feel wrapped in a supportive embrace that empowers you without taking over for you.

Woe to those for whom this song is but an empty echo. Before the night falls, may they find someone who will stand by them, not only in times of peril, but for all times.

*A*ctions

▲ When you needed someone to stand by you has there been someone there for you? Were you willing to ask for support? How did it work out?

▲ Who generally stands by you in times of trouble? Who stands by you every day? Are you thankful for that person? Do you express your thanks? Try to express your gratitude appropriately.

*A*lbum

Anthology; Ben E. King; Rhino R271215.

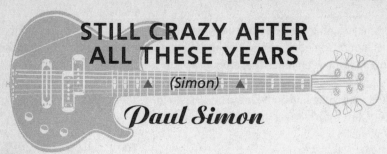

STILL CRAZY AFTER ALL THESE YEARS
▲ *(Simon)* ▲
Paul Simon

Background

Paul Simon is a songwriting kaleidoscope. He soaks up influences like a sponge. From the very beginning of his career, he has exhibited a remarkable gift for incorporating bits and pieces of many styles, many sounds, and many cultures into his work. After the demise of Simon and Garfunkel, he gave free reign to these adventurous impulses, often with astonishing results (for instance, *Graceland*). No matter what stylistic devices he utilizes, there is always at the core of each song the unmistakable voice and vision of Paul Simon. To see what we mean, look no further than the title song of his Grammy winning 1975 album *Still Crazy After All These Years*.

Reflection

All of us have seen obsession portrayed in novels, plays, and films. Some of us have actually experienced it in our own lives. Obsession with an ex-lover can be the subject of amusement, horrifying terror, or, more often, the dull, never ending pain of emptiness and heartbreak.

The loss of the love of your life, especially when you feel it was in some way your fault, can stay with you for a lifetime and ruin your life. Even after you have found someone else, comparison can be devastating and ultimately ruinous of the new love. You can torture yourself endlessly with "What if . . . ?" questions, unmailed letters, and fruitless attempts at contact.

The loss of a love is like a death and must be mourned properly for healing to occur. As in death, there are stages you go through of denial, anger, bargaining, disbelief, and more, but if you allow yourself to feel the pain of the loss beyond blame and second guesses, you will gradually reemerge with some semblance of wholeness.

The keys to recovery are staying in touch with the sources of life for you, including people who love you, and not giving up on yourself. Loss of self-esteem is the frequent companion of this form of rejection and it can send you tumbling on a downward spiral. It can also be the seeds of a new and stronger you and eventually a new relationship that may make you wonder why you were so upset over the loss of the first one.

Actions

If you are trying to get over the loss of a love here are some suggestions:

▲ Deal with your anger in some nondestructive way, like intense physical competition.

▲ If you believe that the breakup was primarily your fault, so be it. Now begin to forgive yourself.

▲ Talk about it to someone who will listen in a nonjudgmental way.

▲ Take the time to deal with your wounds by yourself, but don't drop out. Stay connected to people. Allow yourself to have fun.

▲ Don't jump into a rebound relationship, but gradually begin to dream again and then date again.

Album

Still Crazy After All These Years; Paul Simon; Warner Bro. 255 91-2.

TEACH YOUR CHILDREN

▲ *(Nash)* ▲

Crosby, Stills, Nash and Young

Background

The majority of Crosby, Stills and Nash's top-forty hits have come from the pen of Graham Nash. No doubt about it, those hit-making instincts were forged in his days with the Hollies who placed more than half a dozen singles on the American charts during Nash's tenure with the group. CSN's first taste of top-forty success came with Nash's "Marrakesh Express" in the summer of 1969. He also wrote one of their most beloved songs "Teach Your Children," from the album *Déjà Vu.* It climbed to number sixteen on the singles chart in the summer of 1970. (Next time you hear it, listen for the tasty pedal steel guitar part played by the late Jerry Garcia of the Grateful Dead.)

Reflection

There is so much we want to teach our children, but only so much they are willing to learn from us. Of course, we teach them how to walk and talk, to read and write, and a hundred other things that we may have forgotten as quickly as they learned them. What we are most concerned with teaching them is life, making good choices, having deeply held values, and a spirituality that helps to fulfill them. We also want them to feel good about themselves, to believe in their talents and follow their dreams, and to have a generous and caring heart. It is quite a tall task, one filled with pitfalls, disappointments, and, often, heartbreaks. Somehow, no matter how hard we try, we always have the feeling that we have not done enough and that their failures are our failures as well.

With all the wonderful advice on parenting available in literally hundreds of books and tapes for children from infancy to young adulthood, perhaps the simplest advice is still the wisest. Love them with a generous heart, and let them see in you the model of who and how you want them to be. They will not and should not be that person. They need to be their own person, but they will absorb the best of the values and the spirituality and anything else you share with them in their own way. Just when you may have given up on them learning about life or being able to have a life of their own, they surprise you and you rediscover a little bit of all that good love you gave them coming back to you.

Action

▲ What are the most important things that your parents taught you? Reflect and try to verbalize or write down some key truths, values, or beliefs that they shared with you and how they have affected you. How did they teach best? Were you open to most of what they said or did you resist? What about valuable negative lessons that you learned from them, and swore never to repeat? Have you avoided their pitfalls?

▲ How do you or will you teach your children? Focus on a few most important messages. Are you teaching by example? Are you verbalizing your beliefs and values in a positive way or a nagging, negative, fear-laden harangue? How much of it do you think they get? Keep trying, and don't be discouraged if it seems they aren't getting very much. It is a rare child in a rare moment who shows it that clearly.

Album

Déjà Vu; Crosby, Stills, Nash and Young; Atlantic SD 19118-2.

TEARS IN HEAVEN

▲ *(Clapton/Jennings)* ▲

Eric Clapton

Background

One of the worst tragedies humans must endure in this life is the death of a child. When a parent or grandparent dies, it is very sad, but that is the natural order. The death of a child before his or her time is an affront to that natural order and the source of unimaginable horror and suffering. Eric Clapton endured such a tragedy in 1991, when his four-year-old son Connor fell to his death from the window of a Manhattan apartment building. Working out some of his grief through his music, Clapton wrote a poignant song about Connor called "Tears in Heaven," proving once again that great art can emerge from total tragedy. "Tears In Heaven" won three Grammys in 1993—song of the year, record of the year, and best male pop vocal performance.

Reflection

You are sitting on top of the world and, suddenly, your world falls apart. You are the most respected and admired in your profession, a multimillionaire who can buy what you like and live where you like. Then, your son dies in a tragic accident, and you have to face the sudden, senseless death of a person you would give your life to save. All your money and fame won't help you now, but your faith and creativity will.

Eric Clapton had struggled with the gift and challenge of faith all of his life (see "Let It Grow," p. 124 and "Presence of the Lord," p. 142). Now he used his songwriting talent to tap into the reservoir of faith that is always there if we are open to it. The result was a number-one hit but, more important, a major step in the healing journey for Clapton and his family. It also wound up being a wonderful gift to thousands of other parents who have lost children to death.

You may not be a Grammy-winning singer/songwriter but you can engage your creativity during a time of tragedy, and you can go into that well of faith. If you are a stranger there, you may feel foolish or unworthy. No matter, you will be welcome. It is highly unlikely that you will experience instant relief, nor should you. All you are doing is sowing the seed of hope and eventual healing, but that's not so bad. It will help you to survive. Engaging your talents and creativity in whatever form fits will prevent you from feeling utterly powerless and spinning off into deep depression.

*A*ctions

▲ We hope you will never know the kind of tragedy that Eric Clapton and his family experienced, but the chances are that you will have to deal with death and tragedy in some form. What has been your experience so far? Has any significant healing happened yet for your most recent major losses? How? Who helped?

▲ If you or your loved ones are still in need of healing, where do you go? What or who are the sources of life that help to heal you? Don't be ashamed. Seek them out.

▲ Are you a source of healing for others in these situations, or are you afraid to get involved? What more can you do for someone who has experienced a loss?

*A*lbum

Unplugged; Eric Clapton; Reprise 9 45024-2.

TELL THE TRUTH

▲ *(Clapton/Whitlock)* ▲

Derek and the Dominos

Background

We have mentioned several times Eric Clapton's restless pursuit of the best vehicle for his considerable musical talent. In the late sixties and early seventies, he careened wildly from group to group seeking the perfect musicians to execute his unique artistic vision. He came close once again in 1970 with the release of *Layla and Other Assorted Love Songs* by Derek and the Dominos. Derek was Eric, of course, aided and abetted by Bobby Whitlock, Jim Gordon, Carl Radle, and, in the studio, by the late Duane Allman. Alas, this group, too, fell to pieces in a drug-fueled haze, but the music they made in their all-too-short time together has withstood the test of time, most notably "Layla," "Bell Bottom Blues," "Little Wing," and "Tell the Truth."

Reflection

Truth is the currency of human communication. Without truth, there can be no trust. Without trust there can be no real relationships, neither with lovers, family, friends, partners, teammates, business associates, nor enemies. Without truth you do not know who is your friend or enemy, everyone is under suspicion, everyone is distant. You are alone.

As important as truth is, as much as people nod in assent at its necessity, all too often the nod is not real assent but only passing conformity to what is expected. Students cheat on tests, husbands cheat on wives (and to a lesser extent, vice versa), taxpayers cheat on the government, and government officials cheat to get elected and maintain power. "Everybody does it" is the all-too-convenient excuse for lying.

However, despite this abyss of falsehood, when you experience an untruth aimed at you, a bold-faced lie meant to defame or deceive you, suddenly you know the value and importance of telling the truth and seeking the truth. Without truth, there is chaos, in society and in your own life. As you hear the truth twisted into an endless trail of distortions make sure that the voice you are hearing is not your own. Tell the truth.

*A*ctions

▲ As a rule, do you tell the truth in important matters? Yes? Great!

▲ When do you find it most difficult to tell the truth? What pushes you over the line to lying or cheating?

▲ Try to remember a recent experience in which someone's untruth harmed you or someone you love. How did you feel about it?

▲ How do you deal with people you know who lie to you or distort the truth? Do you let it slide, get angry at them, or challenge them to "rediscover" the truth?

*A*lbum

Layla and Other Assorted Love Songs; Derek and the Dominos; Polydor 847 090-2.

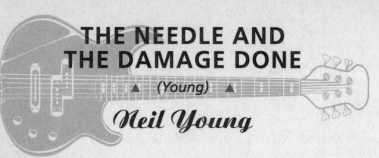

THE NEEDLE AND THE DAMAGE DONE
▲ *(Young)* ▲

Neil Young

Background

Rock 'n' Roll has often been criticized and condemned as "drug music." Certainly, part of this reputation is deserved. The number of songs extolling the virtues of illegal substances coupled with the extraordinary high number of drug-related rock-musician fatalities has reinforced this unfortunate association. That's not the whole story, by any means. For every song that seems to encourage or condone recreational drug use, there is an equal and opposite one that condemns it. Antidrug cautionary tales abound in rock 'n' roll. "Kicks" by Paul Revere and the Raiders, "Undun" by the Guess Who, and "The Pusher" by Steppenwolf come immediately to mind. Who but the musicians who suffered losses caused by drugs are better qualified to comment on their consequences? Such is the case in Neil Young's anguished lament "The Needle and the Damage Done." He put it quite succinctly in the liner notes to the *Decade* anthology, "I am not a preacher, but drugs killed a lot of great men."

Reflection

The numbers of the dead keep increasing, to say nothing of the millions of walking wounded, people whose brains have been scrambled, whose bodies are mere shells, and whose spirits are like listless boats tossed by an ocean too powerful and vast to be overcome.

Millions more, however, have found the safety of the shore through spirit-based programs like Narcotics Anonymous and dozens of similar small-group experiences. Tragically, in many of our most drug-infested cities there are no spots open for addicts who seek help, and most of the federal anti-drug money goes to law enforcement efforts to slow down the influx of drugs pouring into our country.

If you have a problem with drugs or you know someone who does, have hope. The success rate with even hardened drug-addicted criminals is increasing with the right kind of counseling, spirituality, and small community-based support. Yes, there may be damage done in any form of addiction, some of it permanently debilitating, but the human spirit has the strength to rise above the worst and most powerful forms of addictions. The stories are there, human testaments to the courage to overcome hopelessness and the strength of compassionate and steadfast friends, families, counselors and fellow addicts. With all of these success stories, the continuing series of torturous deaths, and our government's failure to adequately support programs that work, is all the more tragic and unacceptable.

Actions

▲ If there is anyone in your life addicted to drugs, including alcohol and tobacco, are you doing all you can to help? Do you know about effective drug or alcohol treatment programs in your community? Are you familiar with the twelve-step programs of Alcoholics Anonymous, Alanon, Alateen, Adult Children of Alcoholics (ACOA), and Narcotics Anonymous? If not, read about them and if you want to help someone who is addicted, go to meetings yourself so you have a sense of how they work.

▲ Is there a skill or a service you can offer to a group in your community that is working on drug prevention and education or drug rehabilitation? Perhaps you can be part of the solution.

▲ Are you part of the problem? Have you developed a need for alcohol or drugs that you know could dominate your life? Remember, needles are not the only way that drugs can cause damage.

Album

Decade; Neil Young; Reprise 2257-2.

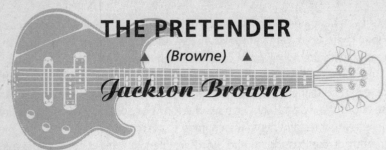

THE PRETENDER
▲ (Browne) ▲
Jackson Browne

*B*ackground

Jackson Browne was no overnight sensation. Years before he made his first appearance on the charts as a recording artist, he was writing songs for a wide range of performers including Tom Rush, Nico, Linda Ronstadt, and the Nitty Gritty Dirt Band. He co-wrote the Eagles' first hit "Take It Easy" in 1972, the same year he released his own solo debut which contained the top-ten hit "Doctor My Eyes." "For Everyman" followed in 1973 and "Late For the Sky" in 1974. It took two years to put together his next album, but it was well worth the wait. "The Pretender" was released in 1976, and became the first of his many platinum-selling albums.

*R*eflection

Is there a fear hidden somewhere inside you that you are a pretender, that your life as other people see you is a sham? "If they really knew me, they would not think I'm so smart or good." "If my partner knew what I was truly like that would be the end of the relationship." The pretender would be unmasked at last. The root cause of this conflict may be a deep-seated insecurity rearing its ugly head, torturing you during the moments of your greatest successes and most satisfying relationships. Doubts swirl around in your mind.

Why is it that sometimes we find it so difficult to accept our own goodness, to be thankful for the good that others see in us, and to appreciate our own finer qualities? It is certainly true that each of us has a darker side. We must face that side of ourselves as well, but not at the expense of denying the love and wisdom and beauty that are ours.

Still, the pretender complex lurks, challenging our achievements and, at times, our very well-being. How to escape its clutches? The first step is to remember that all those good qualities that you may find it hard to accept in yourself are gifts, all of them. Yes, you had something to do with them in that you have accepted them and used them in your life, but they are gifts nevertheless. When you feel good about that part of you, know that it is the best part of you, your true self, your center. When someone affirms you, no need to be shy about it or to appear falsely proud. Just say a sincere thank you and know that there is no pretense, only gratitude.

*A*ctions

▲ Do you have the pretender complex? Do you often feel as though the life you are leading is masking another, less worthy, self? We hope not, because even though some of those tendencies may appear as temptations or even occasional activities, that's not who you are. If the pretender is a frequent visitor in your life, prepare an appropriate departure for a character you do not need.

▲ If there are parts of you that really are the pretender, why do you feel the need to pretend to be someone you are not? There may be many reasons but usually the root cause is insecurity. Fighting that demon is, of course, a lifelong endeavor, but try to revisit some of your more successful accomplishments in this arena, and ask yourself how you can build on them to vanquish the pretender.

*A*lbum

The Pretender; Jackson Browne; Asylum 6E 107-2.

THE PROMISED LAND
▲ *(Springsteen)* ▲

Bruce Springsteen

Background

Sometimes, art and commerce just don't mix. This has been particularly true in rock 'n' roll, where the rebellious nature of the music is often at odds with the profit-driven music business. This simple fact of rock 'n' roll life has affected some of our greatest musical visionaries, including John Fogerty, Tom Petty, and Bruce Springsteen. In Bruce's case, contractual disputes with his former manager put his recording career on hold for three years after the huge success of *Born to Run* in 1975. Bruce did not waste the time, however. He kept visible through extensive touring, and also amassed a huge backlog of songs, many of which were commentaries about the frustrations of dragging art through the marketplace. *Darkness on the Edge of Town* was finally released in 1987 and included the riveting song "The Promised Land."

Reflection

Moses sought the Promised Land most of his adult life. He never made it. He died before the people of Israel entered the Promised Land, but without him they never would have gotten there. What was most important for Moses is what is most important for us. It is the journey, not the destination or the goal. The journey itself, for all of its trials and sufferings, can be a promised land depending on how we travel.

What is the promised land for you? We hope it is more than mere monetary gain, but even if it is some noble pursuit that allows you to use your creativity and talents and makes a positive difference in helping people, your promised land is still more in the journey than the destination.

The millionaire may never see the promised land because he is too busy looking at his stock options and bank accounts. The social activist may not see it because she is lost in one organizing meeting after another. In fact,

most of us will never see it even as we are living in it because we always expect it to be somewhere else or something else. When things are going well,
perhaps especially when they are going well, we focus on what is wrong or
lacking, or which new disaster may befall us instead of living in the joy and
peace of the moment. Some of us believe in a promised land or heaven in the
next life, but for this life it's time to discover the parts of the promised land
that are already here and celebrate them. The rest will be given when we are
ready.

Actions

▲ What does the promised land mean to you? Is it perfection, wealth, sexual fulfillment, power, good health, loving relationships, spiritual insights,
or some combination of all these and more?

▲ What pieces of the promised land are already there in your life? Reflect
on them, savor them, and allow them to play a larger part in your life.

▲ How do you envision the parts of the promised land that are not in your
life: a better job or better health, a new house, a true love, or spiritual en-
lightenment? Having a goal for any of these pieces and working hard
to get them is fine, but don't become so caught up in the journey that
you forget to enjoy it.

Album

Darkness on the Edge of Town; Bruce Springsteen; Columbia CK 35318.

THE SOUNDS OF SILENCE

▲ *(Simon)* ▲

Simon and Garfunkel

Background

It's one of the great legends in rock 'n' roll history that just happens to be the truth. Simon and Garfunkel's 1964 album of folk songs, *Wednesday Morning, 3 A.M.* was a commercial failure. Art went off to graduate school and Paul went off to Europe to perform solo. But then, in 1965, when the folk-rock craze was in full bloom, their producer Tom Wilson added electric bass and drums to one of Paul's songs from the failed album. Columbia released it as a single in the fall of '65. By the end of the year, Art called Paul in Europe and told him to come home in a hurry. Simon and Garfunkel were on the charts and on their way to their very first number-one single—"The Sounds of Silence."

Reflection

Silence rings out ominously when voices should challenge injustice, prejudice, or violence in their midst but are quieted by fear, greed, or some misguided don't-rock-the-boat form of self-preservation. Another malevolent form of silence is an unwelcome visitor at millions of family dinner tables, living rooms, and marital beds. It brings with it boredom, emotional separation, repressed anger, and, sometimes, unreflected hatred. Unless they are challenged and given voice, these silences will grow, as Paul Simon says, like undetected cancers, slowly eating away at couples and families, communities, and whole societies.

What causes these blankets of silence to smother us? Why can't we break the silence that is the spiritual cancer in our relationships with our spouses, children, parents, and siblings? Often, we feel powerless against the silence. When we try to speak, the words become muffled or we get them out without effect. Who will listen? We are resolved to discuss a long, simmering resentment with a loved one but when we try, we only meet a blank wall, no human warmth or willingness to compromise. The silence engulfs us, and gradually it provides an insidious form of comfort. It dulls the passions and deadens the spirit. It quiets opposition or initiative.

Actions

▲ Is there a silence in you that creates a pall-like cover for hurt, disappointment, betrayal, and rage? At times, the silence may save you from doing or saying things you will later regret but it also may be creating distance between you and the people you love. What can you do about the silence in your life?

▲ Do you have a deep-seated resentment about a personal injustice done to you or a loved one by someone or some institution outside your family? Have you kept quiet or has your protest been in vain? What more can you do in a nonviolent way?

Album

Collected Works; Simon and Garfunkel; Columbia C3K 45322.

THE STRANGER
▲ *(Joel)* ▲

Billy Joel

Background

Billy Joel's career achieved new heights with the release of *The Stranger* in 1977. He was already a household name thanks to the success of albums like *Piano Man* and *Turnstiles,* and the singles "Piano Man" and "The Entertainer." But *The Stranger* raised the stakes even higher. No fewer than four of its tracks became big hit singles: "Just the Way You Are," "Movin' Out," "Only the Good Die Young," and "She's Always a Woman." Another two remain staples on FM Radio to this day: "Scenes from an Italian Restaurant" and the haunting title song about the enigmatic stranger.

Reflection

Do you feel sometimes as though an alien being is inhabiting your body and your mind, like you are a spectator at a poorly acted play with characters that you cannot relate to, and the heavy is you? It startles and disturbs you, and worst of all, you have to admit that it is you. You can hardly recognize yourself, but yes, this stranger in your midst is, in fact, a previously undiscovered and certainly unwanted part of yourself.

The great pioneer psychologist Carl Jung called this the *shadow self.* Billy Joel, in one of his most powerful songs, calls it *the stranger.* When this strange cat is finally let out of the bag, how do you deal with it? Jung says it may be another legitimate part of yourself that you have repressed or which has not yet found an appropriate voice, so it intrudes in unexpected ways and inappropriate manners. For example, all of your life you have always put other people first and taken care of them. Now the stranger is saying, "Hey, what about me? Pay attention to my needs as well." Or, have you always been rather proper, but now find yourself being loud, laughing at off-color jokes and getting audibly and visibly angry, where before you would have just let things go?

You say to yourself, "Who is this person?," "This is embarrassing," "What can I do with this unwelcome visitor?" Jung's advice is to get to know this stranger, and value its message and the force within you that it represents. It may be calling you to a better balance, not to radically change your personality in a Jekyll–Hyde manner, but to allow the shadow side, the stranger side, to emerge. Who knows, you may find this stranger to be quite interesting, and eventually become friends.

ctions

▲ There is a difference between characteristics that you do not like about yourself and "the stranger." The stranger is not necessarily the same annoying part of yourself that you have been struggling with for years. More likely, it is the unexpected, out-of-character eruptions that occur from time to time. How do you handle them? How can you tap the vital force that they are without allowing the destructive side to take over?

▲ If you know little pieces of this stranger or shadow self, why not explore further to develop the energy that is trying to get out, but direct it into a positive force in your personality? If the stranger is more aggressive, it could help you to be more assertive. If it is second-guessing you, it could lead you into a more reflective approach to problem solving. The key here is to allow the stranger some room to grow without taking over your personality.

lbum

The Stranger; Billy Joel; CBS CK 34987.

TIME WAITS FOR NO ONE
▲ *(Jagger/Richards)* ▲

The Rolling Stones

Background

Mick Jagger, Keith Richards, and Charlie Watts were, are, and will be, the heart and soul of the Rolling Stones. Ron Wood has been an integral part of the band since 1975. Bill Wyman had a terrific run from the early days right through the Steel Wheels tour in 1989-90. Brian Jones was a founding member of the Stones who died less than one month after leaving the group in the summer of 1969. One last former member deserving acknowledgment is the man who played guitar for the Stones between Jones and Wood—Mick Taylor. Some of his best work for the band can be found on their 1974 album *It's Only Rock 'n' Roll,* in particular, the closing track on side one (when there were sides one and two!) "Time Waits for No One."

Reflection

When we were choosing titles, this one fit in with several related pieces of typical time talk: "Hurry up, time's a-wasting," "You've made it in the nick of time," and "Timing is everything." Respecting time, being in sync with time, valuing time, and not wasting it are all part of the accepted wisdom that most of us have learned. We accept and support all that—most of the time. We want to run a counterplay here, though, because there is a sense in which time does wait for each of us.

The batter who watches a fat pitch right in his powerhouse strike zone may want to kick himself, and so may his manager, but he will get many more pitches like that one. The investor who missed the obvious stock opportunity that would have made her a millionaire will also get another shot. Even the lover who allows the love of his life to slip away and leave him heartbroken will have another opportunity to love again.

Time does wait for no one. It moves on, but it does come around again with new possibilities, new opportunities. The problem is that just as the batter may be so distracted or disheartened by letting that fastball go by that he misses it again, so, too, may we miss opportunities time after time because we are still living in the past with our missed opportunities and bad choices from the first time around. It is understandable that we may get upset with ourselves when we miss important opportunities, but it is absolutely necessary for us to get over it and be ready when time comes our way again with another good one. There is not a scarcity of opportunity; there is an abundance.

*A*ctions

▲ Ask yourself whether past indecision or bad decisions haunt you and become a dead weight that holds you back from making good decisions now?

▲ If you still blame yourself for blowing the big one, the one chance that will never come again, try to get in touch with new possibilities, new chances that are present now.

▲ Don't keep yourself locked into a scarcity of opportunities, rather than the abundance that time and life will really give you. You have to find the key to get yourself out of that prison. In fact, there are several keys, the first one being to learn to forgive yourself and not be so hard on yourself. The other key is to begin to have a change of belief from a scarcity to an abundance of choices. It's real and it's much more fun.

*A*lbum

It's Only Rock 'n' Roll; The Rolling Stones; Rolling Stones Records; Virgin 39500-2-7.

TO KNOW HIM IS TO LOVE HIM

▲ *(Spector)* ▲

The Teddy Bears

*B*ackground

A glance at the charts for the autumn of 1958 is quite revealing. Elvis Presley was represented by a couple of hits from the vaults of RCA, even as the King was serving his country in Germany. The Kingston Trio was spearheading the American folk revival with their number-one single "Tom Dooley." Novelty tunes such as "Beep Beep" by the Playmates, and "The Chipmunk Song" by David Seville were doing quite well. And there were several garden-variety teenage love laments by Ricky Nelson, Conway Twitty, and the Everly Brothers. Then, out of nowhere, at the end of the year, the debut single by a new group called the Teddy Bears shot to the top of the charts and launched the career of a legendary record maker—Phil Spector.

*R*eflection

"To Know Him Is to Love Him" is one of the earliest songs from the rock 'n' roll era chosen for inclusion in this book. There's a very good reason for this that relates directly to the whole notion of rock wisdom. Back in the fifties, if fans even dared to suggest that there might be more to this music than mindless entertainment, they were greeted with scorn and derision. If you liked rock 'n' roll and found yourself in the company of adults, it was always best to just keep your mouth shut.

That all changed for me in the spring of 1959 when a young parish priest in the Bronx, New York, based an entire homily one Sunday morning on the lyrics of "To Know Him Is to Love Him." He suggested that the pronoun in the song's title referred to God. His message was simultaneously simple and profound: Take the time to get acquainted with the Lord and the end result is inescapable—to know Him is to love Him.

It was the first time in my young life that an authority figure made some connection between a rock 'n' roll song and some larger aspect of my existence. It made quite a lasting impression on me. Here's the proof—forty years later, I'm still writing and talking about it. And yes: To know Him (Her) is to love Him (Her)!

*A*ctions

▲ Reflect for a while on the relationship you have with someone you feel you really know. How would you describe your knowing: "We are soul mates," " We have a bond," "We can say anything to each other," "We've been through a lot together," "We always know we will be there for each other"? Rejoice in this relationship! Make sure you tell and show your friend how you feel.

▲ Have you ever said to someone or at least felt like saying, "I used to think I knew you, but now I don't know"? Is there any one thing that broke the bond or did it just seem to happen?

▲ What are the ways that have helped you to really know someone—common interest, deep personal conversations, sharing spirituality, going through a crisis together, sexual intimacy, working on a project together, similar values and dreams?

▲ Do you believe you should have to work at it to know someone deeply, or should it just happen naturally?

▲ What qualities do you need to really know someone—trust, vulnerability, listening, forgiveness, patience, and others? How can you deepen those qualities in yourself?

*A*lbum

Back to Mono; Phil Spector; ABKCO 7118-2.

WAR
▲ (Whitfield/Strong) ▲
Edwin Starr

Background

It is an odd footnote to our nation's musical history, but rock 'n' roll provided the soundtrack for the Vietnam War. Many veterans of the conflict will tell you that the music of the Doors, the Rolling Stones, and Jimi Hendrix accompanied them through the jungles of Southeast Asia. Here on the home front, there was a whole body of music about Vietnam—pro and con. A couple of these songs even made it to the top of the charts. "Ballad of the Green Berets" by Sgt. Barry Sadler was a number-one single in March 1966. Six years later, Motown Artist Edwin Starr topped the charts with "War," a passion-filled plea denouncing the consequences of global conflict. Without specifically mentioning Vietnam, the song nonetheless tapped into the deep frustration and resentment that many loyal Americans felt toward arguably the most controversial war in our nation's history.

Reflection

This song is a diatribe against humankind's most pernicious enemy. Those of us who lived through the Vietnam War saw our friends and relatives come back in body bags, demonstrated against or in support of the war, and still have strong feelings about it. What about our children who grew up after it was over? Their only experience of a U.S. war was watching the high-tech star-wars battle on CNN during the Gulf War. Very few of our troops died. We used weapons of mass destruction to bring the enemy to his knees within a few days. Victory was ours and the cost was not fifty thousand-plus Americans dead. Do our children see war as the horrendous brutal travesty that our parents saw in WW II and the Korean War, that our grandparents knew in WWI, and that we felt in the Vietnam War? Probably not, and that's dangerous. When war seems heroic, relatively painless, righteous, and certain of victory, there is a better chance that it will happen again. Seeing all that old film footage, learning about the sheer terror and overwhelming number of innocent deaths may save us and our grandchildren-to-be from a horror beyond horrors.

*A*ctions

▲ What are your thoughts and feelings now, almost a quarter of a century later, about the Vietnam War?

▲ Does war seem distant to you now, relegated to occasional news stories from other parts of the world that you can hardly pronounce or find on a map?

▲ Have you talked to your children or nieces and nephews about war? What do you say? How do you respond?

▲ Do you ever wonder why we still have a $260 billion plus defense budget long after the breakup of the Soviet Union, at a time when 40 million Americans are without health care and millions more live in deep, dehumanizing poverty?

*A*lbum

Motown Legends: War; Edwin Starr; Essex 8522.

WE CAN WORK IT OUT

▲ *(Lennon/McCartney)* ▲

The Beatles

*B*ackground

Early in their partnership, John Lennon and Paul McCartney agreed to list both of their names on all the songs they wrote, including those they wrote separately. As the world became more and more familiar with their work, it was often obvious which ones were Paul songs and which ones were John songs. Paul's tended to be sweeter, John's harder edged. The chemistry was at its best, however, when John's edginess canceled out some of Paul's sweetness. "We Can Work It Out" is a good example. John explained it in a 1980 interview, "Paul did the first half, I did the middle eight. But you've got Paul writing 'We can work it out,' real optimistic, you know, and me, impatient, 'life is very short and there's no time for fussing and fighting my friend. . . .' " It's just unfortunate that they didn't take their own advice, because then we might have had them around a little bit longer.

*R*eflection

What a wonderful way to approach problem solving or potential disputes! There is a positive presumption that all is possible. The purpose is not confrontation, ego gratification, opponent bashing, or macho posturing. There is an important job to be done, so you both focus on the task, whether it be healing a personal rift, negotiating a complex business deal, or any transaction that could become contentious. You pass up opportunities to take cheap shots, to make paybacks for perceived past injustices, or to score one-upmanship points. There is a bond that brings you both together, a goal to accomplish that invites you despite your differences and it is that goal that is given the spotlight, not any of the emotional baggage that people bring to most disputes or negotiations.

As long as you believe that you can work it out, and put some genuine effort into it, you have a better chance than in most similar situations. When you think about it, life *is* too short for an endless series of squabbles, most of which bring resentment rather than resolution. Yet there are many difficult situations to deal with that can be contentious unless you have the we-can-work-it-out attitude.

*A*ctions

▲ How do you approach most problems with other people? Do you generally focus on opportunities for agreement or on the obstacles? Do you allow the obstacles to seem insurmountable when they may be workable?

▲ Do you tend to be a problem solver, open to the other person's point of view and ready for compromise, or are you more of a blocker, rejecting one proposed solution after another?

▲ How can the we-can-work-it-out attitude help you in personal, business, or social conflicts that you have in your life now?

*A*lbum

Past Masters Volume Two; the Beatles; Parlophone CDP 7 90044 2.

WE GOTTA GET OUT OF THIS PLACE
▲ (Mann/Weil) ▲
The Animals

Background

One of the smartest things the British-invasion bands did was to mine the catalogs of great American rock 'n' roll songwriters for material. The Beatles, the Stones, and the Kinks all did it, so did the Dave Clark Five, Herman's Hermits, and Manfred Mann. Songwriters such as Carole King, Ellie Greenwich, Chuck Berry, and Bob Dylan provided a steady stream of songs for the English bands to repackage and send back to us over the Atlantic. The Animals were certainly not immune to this cross-continental exchange. Most of their best-known songs were penned by Americans in America, and that includes "We Gotta Get Out of this Place," which was written by the legendary husband-and-wife songwriting team, Barry Mann and Cynthia Weil. The Animals' version reached number thirteen in the fall of 1965.

Reflection

This is a very American song. It is what our ancestors said to each other as they left behind famines, wars, religious and political persecution, and grinding poverty. They came here with a belief that they had found a better place that had unlimited possibilities. That belief in progress, in making a better life for yourself and your family, is basic to the American spirit. Many, including these authors, would hold that it is what made America a great country.

It is still possible today. A country boy picks up a guitar and, a few years later, rises to the top of the charts. A ghetto survivor slam dunks his way to a multimillion dollar contract. A very determined woman breaks through the proverbial glass ceiling to become a corporate CEO. A computer nerd creates a series of software packages that propel him to found a billion-dollar software company. Immigrants still come here, work hard, and make their fortunes. The eighties and nineties have seen an explosion of financial superstars with megasalaries. There are 68,000 people who make more than a million dollars a year.

Two problems have emerged with this bonanza. The bottom half of Americans are not in a better place economically. They have slipped badly over the past two decades and, only recently, have begun to creep forward, ever so tenuously. At the same time, the super-rich have gotten much richer and more powerful with a greater influence on society than at any time in the past seventy years. That is not to say that they are all necessarily in a better place emotionally, relationally, or spiritually in their lives. It does say that the gap between them and the rest of us grows larger every year, causing more of us to agree with this song.

Actions

▲ Have you gotten out of a bad financial place or a bad neighborhood? How did it happen? Did you do it by yourself or did you have help? Are you thankful for your success? How do you express that thankfulness? How do you give something back?

▲ Is there another kind of place that you have to get out of—a bad relationship, a dead-end job, the wrong career, an addiction, a dangerous living situation, a depression, or a spiritual desert? Have you actually said the words of this song to someone? Allow them to motivate you to action. Use them as a kind of mantra, believing as our ancestors did that there is a better life for you and those you love.

Album

The Best of the Animals; the Animals; ABKCO 43242.

WHEN A MAN LOVES A WOMAN

▲ *(Lewis/Wright)* ▲

Percy Sledge

Background

Does art reflect life or does life reflect art? It works both ways, of course, and here's a good example of the former. In the midsixties, Percy Sledge was working as a vocalist with the Esquires Combo, a local Alabama group that primarily did cover versions of Beatles' songs and Motown hits. One night on stage, Sledge was so affected by a love affair gone sour that he couldn't bring himself to perform the usual repertoire. Instead, he asked fellow musicians Cameron Lewis and Andrew Wright to improvise something down and dirty. And right there on stage, they worked out the basics to an original song called "When a Man Loves a Woman." Sledge's recorded version came to the attention of executives at Atlantic Records in New York. They released it as a single in early 1966 and, by May 28, it was the number-one song in the country.

Reflection

The blues is one of the basic roots of rock 'n' roll music. It is also a means of catharsis in which the protagonist lets it all hang out, telling a story of woe that usually revolves around being mistreated in love. It becomes a form of therapy for the storyteller who, in sharing the story, also shares the burden, and for the listeners who can relate the pain to their own experiences. Welcome to the blues.

Amazing things happen when a man loves a woman. Most of it is wonderfully crazy, some of it is dangerously on the edge and some of it, as in this song, is over the edge, just plain crazy.

This is definitely one of those she-done-him-wrong songs, and because of the temporary blindness that love often imposes, he is the last one to see that she played him for a fool. Even though he would have turned his back on his best friend for her, spent his last dime, given up all his comforts, and even slept out in the rain, it wasn't enough. Does this all sound strange? It is, but it's not unusual. You have probably heard a version of this story many times in real life and wondered how anyone would be so foolish—until it happens to you.

*A*ctions

▲ If you know someone who is in an emotionally abusive relationship or has been betrayed but doesn't see it, try to help that person see what is really going on. Make sure you are certain of the facts and then provide a supportive challenge to your friend to face up to a very painful reality. Do not be surprised if you meet resistance at first.

▲ Are you in this kind of relationship? Why do you stay? Is there something that you are getting out of the relationship? Whatever it is, you can do without it. What are you afraid of if you leave the relationship? Face your fears, get the protection and support you need, and make the move.

*A*lbum

Best Of; Percy Sledge; Atlantic 8210.

WILL YOU LOVE ME TOMORROW?
▲ *(Goffin/King)* ▲
The Shirelles

*B*ackground

Carole King is unquestionably one of the most significant and successful women in the history of male-dominated rock 'n' roll. Putting aside her enormously productive career as a vocalist and performer for the moment, her songwriting credentials alone earned her a well-deserved place in the Rock and Roll Hall of Fame. Carole and her first husband Gerry Goffin collaborated on an incredible number of top-forty hits during the sixties including chart-toppers such as "Take Good Care of My Baby," "The Locomotion," and "Go Away Little Girl." Their first number one was the Shirelles' terrific recording of "Will You Love Me Tomorrow"—a very sophisticated song for 1961, indeed!

*R*eflection

When you think of the sixties you immediately think of the sexual revolution, right in the same breath as the Kennedy assassinations, Dr. Martin Luther King and the civil-rights movement, and the Vietnam War. This song was released in 1960, long before any of those events made their mark on history. It was at one and the same time a glimpse into the past sexist relationships that existed between men and women, and a glimpse into the future and the ever increasing freedom people would experience in premarital sexual relationships.

Can you imagine a guy singing this song? What a joke! In the old sexual stereotype that unfortunately is still with us, the man can have any number of one-night stands or short-term relationships. In the past it was said that he was sowing his wild oats. Today it might be said he is performing his rite of passage, becoming a man. It's different for a woman. She is losing her virginity, being a fast girl or a tramp. This song confronts the stereotypes and asks a question that most women but few men ask themselves before hopping into bed, "Will you love me tomorrow?" The assumption somehow is that he might see her in a less favorable light. He might have gotten what he wanted, and then move on. Hey guys, wake up! Do we think that the double standard is actually good for anyone, man or woman?

Actions

▲ Do you think that sexual morality should be different for a man than a woman? If you don't think or believe that way on an intellectual level, does a part of you still feel that way? If so, try to get in touch with where that feeling comes from in your background and how it influences you now.

▲ What questions do you ask yourself, what requirements do you have, what values come into play before you have sex with a new partner?

▲ Try to recall past first times with previous partners. Did you love the person more or less the next day, or did love play no part in the encounter?

Album

Billboard Top Rock 'n' Roll Hits 1961; Various Artists; Rhino R2 70622.

WITH A LITTLE HELP FROM MY FRIENDS

▲ *(Lennon/McCartney)* ▲

The Beatles

Background

Even though Ringo Starr was the oldest Beatle (he was born three months before John Lennon in 1940), he was always treated like a younger brother by his more prolific bandmates. They watched out for him. They protected him. They made sure that each album and each concert contained a few moments that were uniquely Ringo. "Boys," "I Want to Be Your Lover," "Act Naturally," and "Yellow Submarine" all placed Ringo squarely in the spotlight. The greatest example of John, Paul, and George's affection and generosity of spirit toward Ringo occurred on their masterpiece *Sgt. Pepper's Lonely Hearts Club Band*. After establishing their alternate personas in the title track of this free-wheeling concept album, it is Ringo who takes center stage to sing the song that instantly became his own personal Beatle theme song—"With a Little Help from My Friends."

Reflection

Self-reliance is one of the great American traits. We believe in self-help, pulling yourself up by your bootstraps, getting the job done. The truth is, however, that we do need a little, and sometimes a great deal, of help from our friends. There is something inside of us that desperately wants to be independent, but sometimes it is not enough.

Reaching out to a friend and receiving help is one of the most gratifying and healing experiences in life, but it can only happen if you have friends and you are willing to ask for help. Unfortunately, in our society rootlessness is a major problem for many young people. They finish school, where they may have had a good network of friends and family, and then move away to find work or to find themselves.

What they often find instead is loneliness, a feeling of disconnection from any kind of nurturing relationships, and the danger of settling for acquaintances instead of real friends. This pattern can also develop during middle age and, of course, in old age when friends die or move away to retire.

The other problem is in accepting help when you have been taught you should do it all yourself. That's the dark side of self-reliance. Sometimes it takes the form of shyness, at other times it appears as a kind of stubbornness. Whatever its manifestation, it tends to prevent you from asking for the kind of help you need. The answer is to take what we call a reasoned risk. Reach out to the person that you believe will be most receptive and most capable of helping. Part of your decision will be based on a process of figuring all the possibilities as best you can, but part of it will also come from intuition, following your best instinct. However, if your first shot at help-seeking comes up empty, or worse, ends in a rejection, don't give up. Refocus yourself and try again.

*A*ctions

▲ Do you ask friends for help when you really need it? If so, how does it usually work out? Do they come through for you or do they let you down? If someone lets you down do you give up, or try someone else who may be more suited? If you need the help of a friend now, focus on which friend to ask and how. Then do it!

▲ Are you there for your friends or are you too busy, distracted, or self-focused to respond effectively? Ask yourself how you can be more tuned in to appeals for help from your friends. Sometimes the hardest request to discern is simply to listen without passing judgment.

▲ There is often a problem of abusing a friendship by asking for help that is inappropriate or asking in an inappropriate way. Is anyone doing that to you or are you doing it to someone? What can you do to correct the situation without harming the friendship?

*A*lbum

Sgt. Pepper's Lonely Hearts Club Band; The Beatles; Parlophone CDP 46442 2.

WON'T GET FOOLED AGAIN

▲ *(Townshend)* ▲

The Who

*B*ackground

How do you top an amazing accomplishment like the rock opera *Tommy* by the Who? That was the daunting challenge facing composer Pete Townshend at the beginning of the seventies. He bought some time by releasing a live album (*The Who Live at Leeds*), then hunkered down to the serious task of putting together a new LP of original songs for release in 1971. *Who's Next* didn't just equal *Tommy;* in some respects, it surpassed it. To this day it is regarded as one of the greatest rock albums of all time and with good reason: The songs are uniformly brilliant, the performances are stellar, and the overall production is powerful and unrelenting. A huge commercial success and a unanimous critical triumph, *Who's Next* yielded no less than two of rock 'n' roll's greatest anthems—"Baba O'Riley" and "Won't Get Fooled Again."

*R*eflection

"Won't get fooled again." How may times have you said that, only to find later that you did get fooled again? You said to yourself, how can I make that same mistake over and over again? How can I be so gullible and be taken in again? How can I fall for good looks and wind up with a mean spirit again? How can I even imagine that I can take that one drink, that one smoke, make that one bet again? How can I trust after I have been betrayed again and again? When will I learn?

On the one hand, don't be too hard on yourself. When you get too down on yourself, you are more likely to get fooled again or make the same mistake repeatedly. It is a truism that everybody makes mistakes. What you may not realize is that most people make mistakes in bunches—often the same mistake.

On the other hand, you do need to learn from your mistakes. If you have been fooled again by a trusted friend, family member, or lover, you need to make different decisions about that person and not be as vulnerable. One possibility is a major confrontation in which you have it out. Another is to absorb the hostility or betrayal and try to rebuild the relationship. Sometimes, either approach is appropriate but there are other options, including nonviolent challenge. You say not only what you think but how you feel. You try to convey what you believe to be the truth about the situation and how it is affecting you, the pain it has caused you. You stay open to hear the other person's side and yet be steadfast in your response. Sometimes, you will get some satisfaction. The truth will come from the other person, and it will help to heal the relationship. At other times, you may learn something that you did not fully understand before that puts the whole matter in a different light. Or, it may push you further apart because there is no admission of fault or responsibility. Then, for sure, don't be fooled again.

*A*ctions

▲ When did you really get fooled again, when you definitely should have known better? Have you done anything to make sure it doesn't happen again?

▲ Have you found that sometimes you have overreacted when you got fooled again? Perhaps you have closed your mind to something, or worse, closed your heart because you have been hurt? That may have been appropriate to protect yourself for a while, but has it put up a permanent wall around your heart? Maybe it's time to let down the walls a bit, without getting fooled again.

*A*lbum

Who's Next; The Who; MCA MCAD-11269.

YOU CAN'T ALWAYS GET WHAT YOU WANT

▲ *(Jagger/Richards)* ▲

The Rolling Stones

Background

The Rolling Stones have been a part of our lives for almost four decades. It is hard to imagine the world without them. It is impossible to imagine rock 'n' roll without them. Their music is intimately intertwined with the most public events or our collective history, as well as the most private moments of our personal lives. This mythic power was illustrated beautifully in the eighties movie *The Big Chill*. As the ensemble cast gathers for the funeral service of a deceased friend, the organist launches into the unmistakable opening notes of "You Can't Always Get What You Want." The original recorded version appeared on the *Let It Bleed* album in November 1969.

Reflection

You work hard to get the dream job of a lifetime. You do and say all the right things. They even offer you the job, but then the whole deal falls through. Depressed is too gentle a word to describe how you feel. After a while though, you find an even better job and you breathe a sigh of relief that you did not land the first one.

You fall in love with a gorgeous, intelligent, wonderful person, who eventually leaves you for someone else. A year later you meet the person that is the right person for you, you get married and have a happy life together . Another close call! Perhaps you have not had an experience quite that dramatic but, more than likely, you have had several experiences in which you had your heart and mind and energies set on achieving something, only to come up empty . Sometimes, it is simply a disappointing experience but occasionally there is something else on the horizon that is better, more suitable for you, if only you stay open and not too wiped out by the original failure.

What you want and what you need are often very different realities. We live in an age of instant gratification: "I want it and I want it now." If you look a little bit closer, you just might find that many of your greatest accomplishments and most fulfilling relationships did not come directly from your efforts. You tried hard, but what you got was not what you wanted. Somehow, though, it turned out to be what you really needed and now cherish.

*A*ctions

▲ Reflect for a while on all that is most precious to you: your relationships, talents, successes, and outstanding qualities. How many came about as a result of you wanting them and working hard for them, and how many came to you indirectly, as gifts, because you needed them?

▲ Is there a situation in your life right now in which you have tried hard for something without apparent success? Could it be that this is not really what you need? Perhaps there is another possibility for receiving what you need if you are open to it. Allow yourself to be more available to other options, other gifts in the face of frustration or failure.

*A*lbum

Let It Bleed; The Rolling Stones; ABKCO 80042.

YOU CAN'T HURRY LOVE

▲ *(Holland/Dozier/Holland)* ▲

The Supremes

Background

The Supremes were a virtual hitmaking machine for Motown, but it didn't start out that way. Originally know as the Primettes (the Temptations had evolved from a group called the Primes), Diana Ross, Florence Ballard, and Mary Wilson released eight singles without success before recording "Where Did Our Love Go" in 1964. The song went to the top of the charts, and began an unprecedented string of five singles in a row that went straight to number one. The other four were "Baby Love," "Come See About Me," "Stop in the Name of Love," and "Back in My Arms Again." Two years later, the group was still practicing their effortless hitmaking ways. "You Can't Hurry Love" went straight to number one in September 1966.

Reflection

There are certain pieces of wisdom that we learn from our parents at an early age which stay with us for a lifetime. They are a comfort, a warning, or an incentive to us in times of crisis or disappointment. Perhaps your mother or father told you that you "can't hurry love," but, if not, you can hear it loud and clear from Diana Ross. This one insight is so important that it can literally save your life, and certainly keep you from a great deal of unnecessary pain.

Every one of us wants to love and be loved in the deepest, most complete way. As we reach adolescence and young adulthood we may assume that it will just happen. As the years pass, it doesn't or we think it has and then, after a while, the relationship falls apart and we are left alone again. This can lead to desperation and a series of bad choices or to a depressing kind of loneliness that seems to lead nowhere.

You may have a different love clock than your partner. You may want to move more slowly or more quickly in revealing yourself, in trust, or in sexual intimacy, living together, and marriage. It is important to know just what your love clock is and why it works at that speed and to understand the workings of your lover's. Part of the difference has to do with overall personality but another important factor revolves around issues of self-esteem and neediness. You hope that your lover is ready to move onto the next level of the relationship when you are. Not too likely! So go back to that reassuringly wise admonition, "you can't hurry love," and reflect on what it means for your relationship.

*A*ctions

▲ Do you feel rushed by your partner? You love this person but things are moving too fast. Share your feelings. Try to make sure that you do not come across as negative or rejecting, but say it.

▲ If you are the person trying to move the relationship along and you are meeting some resistance, try to be clear about your own motivations for pressing the issues. At the same time, identify the reasons for the resistance. Begin by tactfully asking the causes of the reluctance to take the next step. If you really believe this relationship is the one, be patient—up to a point.

▲ If there is no deep relationship in your life, take some positive steps to become connected with the kind of people you want to meet, rather than being passive or looking in places that you know will be trouble. But always remember: "You can't hurry love."

*A*lbum

Anthology; The Supremes; Motown 314-530511-2.

YOU DON'T OWN ME

▲ *(Madara/White)* ▲

Lesley Gore

Background

When the definitive history of the feminist movement in the United States is written, Lesley Gore, at the very least, deserves a footnote. Known primarily for teen hits such as "It's My Party," "Judy's Turn to Cry," and "She's a Fool," Gore, a middle-class teenager from Tenafly, New Jersey, brought to the charts what can easily be considered the first feminist anthem. "You Don't Own Me" became a number-two single in early 1964. (The only thing keeping it from number one was the early explosion of Beatlemania.) In a musical form that routinely exploited and objectified women, Gore's defiant proclamation of independence was an early warning sign of what was to come later in the decade.

Reflections

The words of this song are as powerful and relevant today as they were thirty-four years ago when Lesley Gore first sang them. Isn't that a shame? Isn't it shocking that after all these years and with the presence of the women's movement men still create trophy wives and girlfriends, and still try to dominate and control women? Sexism is being chipped away little by little, and great victories have been won, but women still face discrimination and oppression. It comes not only from strangers in the workplace but even more insidiously from their husbands, boyfriends, and male relatives.

Even the famed sexual revolution was a two-edged sword. It has given women more freedom over their own bodies and challenged the very stereotypes in this song but it has also left them more vulnerable to potential abuse and date rape. As long as advertising and the media portray women as sex objects to be possessed rather than multidimensional subjects, persons to be loved, respected, and treated equally, there will always be the temptation for men to try to own this precious treasure. What many men fail to realize is that to the extent that they dehumanize women in any way, they are also de-humanizing themselves. What could have been a union of two free, total persons is instead no more than an arrangement in which both use each other and both come up the losers.

$\mathcal{A}$ctions

▲ If you are a man, ask yourself whether you are guilty of any of the actions and attitudes in this song. If so, what can you do to change?

▲ If you are a woman, how do you deal with sexism in the workplace, in your family, and in relationships? Have you learned how to confront sex-ist comments or behavior in a positive way, or are you still afraid of risk-ing the loss of a job or of someone's self-esteem?

▲ If you have children, what are you teaching them about gender equal-ity and mutual respect and, more important, how are you modeling your beliefs?

$\mathcal{A}$lbum

Golden Hits of Lesley Gore; Lesley Gore; Mercury CD 810370-2.

YOU'RE SO VAIN

▲ *(Simon)* ▲

Carly Simon

Background

Carly Simon already had a couple of top-forty hits under her belt when "You're So Vain" was released as a single from her *No Secrets* album. It went to number one in January 1973. The song had a lot going for it. Mick Jagger contributed background vocals. Richard Perry (who had tremendous success with artists as diverse as Harry Nilsson, Ringo Starr, and Barbra Streisand) produced it. Then there was the guessing game that the song triggered. Who was it about? Jagger? James Taylor? Warren Beatty? Carly herself has never publicly revealed the identity of her self-involved mystery man. But one thing is for sure. Somebody did her dirty, and Carly didn't get mad, she got even!

Reflection

You've met this person, probably several times in your life. They act as if they are the center of the universe. All else must stop and focus on the words, deeds, stories, problems, complaints, and triumphs of this obnoxious and sad individual. What causes such a noxious malady?

Almost without exception, glaringly vain people are also pathetically insecure people, but they have developed clever and often devious disguises for their insecurity. Endless inside stories of movie, sports, and rock stars, political powerhouses, and multimillionaire CEOs confirm this truth.

Whatever talent, power, or possessions they have, they flaunt to excess because it gives them a sense of security or meaning, no matter how false or hollow it may be. Vain people have never experienced a deep sense of self-worth. They have bought into our society's competitive, materialistic values, and believe they will be judged not for who they are but for their latest achievements and position. Their lives become a theater to showcase their latest accomplishments, and to put down any serious rivals. There is an almost instant cure for this disease. It is real love and friendship. It's a long road back when a vain person begins to be accepted and honored just because of who they are, but, at least, the cure has been set in motion.

*A*ctions

▲ How do you deal with an especially vain person who is a regular part of your life? Do you confront, cajole, or simply ignore the vanity?

▲ Have you experienced the effective transformation of a vain person? How did it happen?

▲ As you teach your children, how do you help them to have a good sense of self-esteem without giving them a swelled head?

*A*lbum

No Secrets; Carly Simon; Elektra 75049-2.

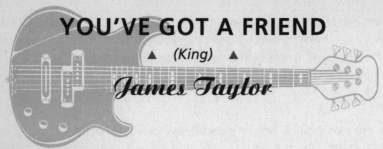

YOU'VE GOT A FRIEND

▲ *(King)* ▲

James Taylor

*B*ackground

Carole King once told me that "You've Got a Friend" was one of those songs that just seemed to come through her from someplace else. She sat down at the piano and it just poured out. Carole certainly lived up to the spirit of the song by sharing it with James Taylor. The two met through a mutual friend and collaborator Danny Kortchmar. After James became a huge star in 1971, he asked Carole to be his opening act on a twenty-seven-city tour of America. Meanwhile, Carole became a star in her own right after the release of *Tapestry*, which included "You've Got a Friend." James recorded it, released it as a single, and it went to number one in July 1971. On Grammy night the following year, the two friends shared the glory—James for Best Pop Male Vocal Performance and Carole for Song of the Year.

*R*eflection

You might think the sentiments in this song are about as good as it gets when it comes to friendship. If you have this kind of friendship with anyone, you have a truly great gift. Your friends will be there for you anytime, anyplace, at your call. There are heroic dimensions to this friendship, great sacrifices, extreme generosity. What more can you ask?

Abiding presence! On a whole other level, that's what friendship is all about. It may include heroic sacrifices and last-minute saving interventions, but most of the time it is an abiding presence that does not need to be called upon, it simply is. There is a level of depth, intimacy, and trust that is pervasive.

Is this a fantasy friendship or does it exist in real life? The better question is, does it exist in your life? People who have this kind of relationship did not come by it without great risk, sacrifice, disappointment, and suffering. If you open yourself on this level, there is no doubt you will get hurt in one way or another, but the benefits far outweigh the costs (we thought we would throw that in for all you bottom-line business types). On the one hand, there is a peace of mind and comfort in this friendship, on the other hand, there is a companion for adventure into the depths of the spirit and the breadth of life.

*A*ctions

▲ What do you mean when you say "my good friend"? What qualities do you see in the relationship?

▲ Do you consider yourself to be a good friend? Are you willing to sacrifice for your friend, to be there and listen?

▲ How do you deal with the loss of a friend, for any reason? Do you retreat into yourself or do you become more open to another person who could become a good friend?

▲ Is there someone in your life who is the abiding-presence kind of friend for you?

*A*lbums

Greatest Hits; James Taylor; Warner Brothers 3113-2. *Tapestry;* Carole King; Ode EK 34946.

YOU'VE LOST THAT LOVING FEELING

▲ *(Mann/Weil/Spector)* ▲

The Righteous Brothers

Background

A remarkable thing happened in 1997. "You've Lost That Loving Feeling" by the Righteous Brothers surpassed "Yesterday" by the Beatles as the most-played song on American radio in broadcasting history. That's quite an accomplishment, and all the credit for it must be spread out evenly among the song's composers, producers, and performers. It was written by the famous husband-and-wife songwriting team of Barry Mann and Cynthia Weil with a little help from Phil Spector. Spector also produced the track using his legendary wall-of-sound technique. And, finally, the song was performed by the foremost practitioners of what came to be known as *blue-eyed soul*—Bill Medley and Bobby Hatfield, the Righteous Brothers. Given that extraordinary pedigree, "You've Lost That Loving Feeling" went straight to the top of the charts in February of 1965.

Reflection

How did it happen? Did you wake up one morning and suddenly find it gone? Did it slowly, painfully, slip away into the lost recesses of past passion? Or can you point to that moment in time when it was mortally wounded by a seemingly irreversible betrayal, abandonment, or other despicable deed? In any case, you have lost it, or perhaps your lover has lost it for you.

There is a deep sadness when a love is lost, no matter how it happens, but sometimes the circumstances make the loss especially devastating. You never saw it coming, you missed all the signs. You don't want it to end, and you feel powerless to do anything to reclaim what once was. The loss has precipitated a lengthy depression or catapulted you into a series of bad decisions with disastrous consequences.

But stop! Did you really lose that loving feeling or is it just a different feeling? Sometimes a love that is largely one-dimensional loses some of the power of that dimension, for example, sexual passion, but holds the promise for deeper possibilities. At other times, the changes or growth happening in one person seem like a threat to the other but need not be. Make sure that the loving feeling is genuinely lost before you give up. Love has many faces. A new one might smile at you as the other disappears. There may be some ways you have not yet discovered that can bring back that loving feeling. If you have had a deep genuine love, it is worth trying again.

*A*ctions

▲ If you've lost that loving feeling ask yourself why. What part of it is your responsibility? Is it connected to past rejections or abuses? Have you misguided or misunderstood your lover? Is there still some loving feeling on your part? Do you feel anything coming back to you? If so, all may not be lost.

▲ If someone has lost it for you, and you have tried to heal the relationship without success, focus instead on healing yourself. The loss may be so excrutiating, and you may be so angry or down on yourself, that you do not recognize your need for healing. Wake up! Do not allow yourself to wallow in self-pity. No matter what mistakes you have made, you do deserve healing. Give yourself a break, learn from the experience, and go forward.

*A*lbum

Back to Mono; Phil Spector; ABKCO 7118-2.

YOU'VE MADE ME SO VERY HAPPY

(Gordy/Holloway/Holloway/Wilson)

Blood, Sweat and Tears

Background

Any discussion of Blood, Sweat and Tears must begin with the multitalented arranger, composer, performer, and producer, Al Kooper. After the breakup of The Blues Project in the late sixties, it was Kooper's vision to put together a group that combined the best aspects of folk, rock, and blues with jazz. All of these elements coalesced on BS&T's debut album, *Child is Father to the Man*, in 1968. The record was an instant FM favorite, but only enjoyed modest commercial success. Kooper moved on to other projects, and the band re-grouped around Canadian vocalist David Clayon-Thomas. Their self-titled second album refined some of the rough edges of their debut and capitalized on the vocal strengths of Clayton-Thomas. The result was instantly success-ful, yielding three top-ten singles. The first of these was a remake of Brenda Holloway's "You've Made Me So Very Happy" which climbed to number two on the charts in April 1969.

Reflection

Is it really possible to make another person happy? You can give all kinds of pleasure and even momentary happy feelings to people. People may sin-cerely say they are happy that you are in their lives. But are you really making someone happy, or unhappy, for that matter? Isn't happiness something that comes from inside? There are certainly many factors from the outside that af-fect happiness. The question is, who makes you happy, you or others?

The truth is no one can make you happy, only you, but many people can contribute to your happiness, or help destroy it. Your parents can be nurtur-ing or abusive, your teachers creative and concerned or boring and de-tached, your friends supportive or disloyal, your significant other loving and affirming or a growing menace to your physical, spiritual, and mental well-being. The key to happiness is the choices you make and how you live with them. You can choose to associate yourself with positive, lifegiving people or deep down you can believe that you are not worthy of such goodness and settle for friends and associates who are not really in your best interest. You can choose to leave a destructive relationship, or be passive to its dangers and suffer internally. You can take a risk and try to make new friends and ac-quaintances or retreat into yourself, believing that they will either reject or otherwise harm you. You can become so self-absorbed that everything re-volves around you, you can lose your selfhood in taking care of others, or you can be open to both giving and receiving love, support, and friendship. No one can make you happy but you can accept the gift of happiness others offer you and you can, in turn, offer it to others. Happiness is one of the few things, like love, that you never lose when you give it away.

Actions

▲ Do you feel alive and positive when you wake up each day, or is it a chore to get out of bed? How about at the end of the day, do you feel at peace with yourself? If your answer is overwhelmingly negative to both of those questions, you may be suffering from depression. The good news is that there is help available—ask for it.

▲ Think about the most important people in your life as well as the people with whom you spend the most time (not necessarily the same people). As best you can tell, which have a more positive, happy approach to life? How can you spend more time with them?

▲ Do you find you always need to be around people to make you happy, or are you able to be happy when you spend time by yourself, by choice?

Album

Blood, Sweat and Tears; Blood, Sweat and Tears; Columbia CK 9720.